UNDERSTANDING THE IMPORTANCE OF PERSONAL FINANCE

Introduction

Personal finance is a crucial aspect of our lives that often receives inadequate attention and consideration. It encompasses managing one's money, budgeting, saving, investing, and making informed financial decisions to achieve financial goals and secure a stable future. Understanding the importance of personal finance is paramount for individual well-being, financial stability, and overall quality of life. This essay aims to elucidate the significance of personal finance and its impact on an individual's life.

Financial Security and Stability

One of the fundamental reasons why understanding personal finance is essential is to attain financial security and stability. By managing income, expenses, and debt responsibly, individuals can create a safety net that protects them from unforeseen circumstances such as medical emergencies, job loss, or accidents. Proper financial planning helps in building an emergency fund, ensuring that unexpected expenses do not jeopardize financial stability.

Goal Achievement and Aspirations

Personal finance acts as a roadmap to achieve both short-term and long-term financial goals. Whether it's buying a house, starting a business, traveling the world, or retiring comfortably, financial planning is the key. Understanding how to budget, save, invest, and manage debt enables individuals to set realistic goals and work towards achieving them. With prudent financial decisions, individuals can fulfill their aspirations and lead a fulfilling life.

Debt Management and Avoidance

Understanding personal finance equips individuals with the knowledge to manage and avoid debt effectively. Debt can quickly spiral out of control, leading to financial stress and instability. Personal finance educates individuals about responsible borrowing, how to pay off debts efficiently, and how to avoid unnecessary debt. By being cognizant of their financial situation, individuals can maintain a healthy debt-to-income ratio and avoid financial burdens.

Wealth Building and Retirement Planning

Personal finance is a cornerstone for wealth building and retirement planning. Through smart investment strategies and long-term financial planning, individuals can grow their wealth over time. This growth in wealth ensures a comfortable retirement, where one can maintain their lifestyle and pursue their interests without financial worries. Starting early and making informed investment decisions can significantly impact the amount of wealth an individual accumulates for their retirement years.

Financial Literacy and Empowerment

Understanding personal finance enhances financial literacy and empowers individuals to make informed financial decisions. Knowledge about concepts like compound interest, inflation, diversification, and risk management allows individuals to assess financial products and investments critically. This, in turn, helps in making choices that align with their financial goals and risk tolerance.

Conclusion

Understanding the importance of personal finance is paramount for achieving financial security, realizing life goals, managing debt, building wealth, and making informed financial decisions. Financial literacy equips individuals with the tools and knowledge needed to navigate the complex world of finance successfully. By investing time and effort in understanding personal finance, individuals can shape a brighter and more secure financial future for themselves and their families.

SETTING FINANCIAL GOALS AND OBJECTIVES

Introduction

Setting financial goals and objectives is a fundamental step in establishing a path towards financial stability, security, and overall well-being. Goals provide direction, motivation, and a sense of purpose in managing one's finances effectively. By defining clear financial objectives, individuals can better understand their financial situation, prioritize their needs and wants, and work towards achieving a more secure financial future. This essay elaborates on the importance of setting financial goals and objectives and the positive impact it has on an individual's financial journey.

Clarity and Direction

Financial goals provide individuals with a clear direction for their financial journey. They act as a roadmap, guiding actions and decisions towards achieving specific outcomes. Whether it's saving for a down payment on a house, funding a child's education, or planning for retirement, having well-defined financial objectives enables individuals to set achievable targets and create a step-by-step plan to reach them.

Motivation and Discipline

Setting financial goals and objectives instills motivation and discipline in managing finances. Knowing what one is working towards motivates individuals to make better financial choices, save more, spend wisely, and stay focused on their goals. Discipline plays a crucial role in adhering to a budget, controlling impulsive spending, and maintaining a consistent saving and investment regimen, all of which are essential for achieving financial objectives.

Prioritization and Allocation

Financial goals help in prioritizing financial needs and wants. By establishing goals, individuals can discern what is most important to them and allocate resources accordingly. This aids in striking a balance between immediate needs and future aspirations. Proper allocation of resources ensures that essential goals are met without compromising the ability to achieve long-term financial objectives.

Financial Security and Resilience

Setting financial goals contributes significantly to financial security and resilience. Emergency funds, insurance coverage, and debt reduction are common financial goals that enhance an individual's ability to navigate unexpected financial challenges. By having these goals in place, individuals can better prepare for unexpected events and secure themselves and their families against financial setbacks.

Long-Term Financial Growth

Financial objectives often encompass long-term goals such as buying a home, funding education, or retiring comfortably. These objectives encourage individuals to invest wisely, save consistently, and plan for the future. By setting these long-term goals, individuals can harness the power of compounding and asset appreciation, ensuring long-term financial growth and sustainability.

Monitoring and Adjusting

Setting financial goals is an ongoing process that requires regular monitoring and adjustment. Individuals should periodically review their progress, reassess their goals, and make necessary adjustments based on changing circumstances, financial status, or priorities. This adaptability ensures that financial goals remain relevant and achievable over time.

Conclusion

Setting financial goals and objectives is a pivotal step towards financial success and security. It provides clarity, direction, motivation, and discipline, allowing individuals to manage their finances more effectively. By prioritizing needs, allocating resources, and planning for the future, individuals can achieve both short-term and long-term financial objectives, ultimately leading to a more secure and fulfilling financial life. Regular monitoring and adjustments ensure that goals remain relevant and attainable, leading to sustained financial growth and prosperity.

EVALUATING YOUR FINANCIAL HEALTH

Introduction

Evaluating one's financial health is a crucial step toward achieving financial well-being and stability. Financial health encompasses various aspects of an individual's financial situation, including income, expenses, debt, savings, investments, and overall financial management. Understanding and assessing one's financial health helps in identifying strengths, weaknesses, opportunities, and threats in one's financial life. This essay elaborates on the importance of evaluating financial health and provides insights into how individuals can assess and improve their financial well-being.

Understanding Financial Health

Financial health refers to the overall state of an individual's financial affairs and their ability to manage and sustain their finances over time. It encompasses multiple dimensions, such as liquidity, solvency, financial behavior, and financial resilience. Evaluating financial health involves analyzing income levels, spending habits, debt management, savings, investments, and the ability to plan for the future.

Importance of Evaluating Financial Health

1. **Identifying Strengths and Weaknesses**: Evaluating financial health helps in identifying areas where an individual is financially strong, such as a high savings rate or low debt levels, and areas that need improvement, such as excessive spending or inadequate savings.

2. **Setting Realistic Goals**: Understanding one's financial health is crucial for setting realistic financial goals. It allows individuals to align their goals with their current financial capacity and develop a viable plan to achieve them.

3. **Risk Management**: Assessing financial health aids in identifying potential financial risks and vulnerabilities. It allows individuals to take appropriate measures to mitigate risks, such as securing insurance coverage or diversifying investments.

4. **Budgeting and Spending Control**: By evaluating income and expenses, individuals can create a comprehensive budget that guides spending and ensures that expenses are within means. This promotes better financial discipline and aids in achieving financial objectives.

5. **Debt Management**: Understanding one's financial health involves assessing debt levels and repayment capacity. This knowledge is vital for formulating a strategy to manage and pay off debt efficiently.

6. **Long-Term Financial Planning**: A clear understanding of financial health enables long-term financial planning, including retirement planning, wealth building, and legacy planning. It ensures that individuals are on track to achieve their long-term financial objectives.

Evaluating Financial Health: Key Metrics and Indicators

1. **Net Worth**: Calculating net worth (assets minus liabilities) provides a snapshot of an individual's overall financial position.

2. **Cash Flow Analysis**: Analyzing income and expenses helps in understanding spending patterns and identifying potential areas for savings.

3. **Debt-to-Income Ratio**: This ratio assesses an individual's debt burden compared to their income and helps in managing debt effectively.

4. **Emergency Fund Adequacy**: Assessing the sufficiency of an emergency fund helps in ensuring financial resilience in the face of unexpected expenses or emergencies.

5. **Savings Rate**: Evaluating the proportion of income saved each month gives insight into an individual's ability to save for the future.

Conclusion

Evaluating financial health is an essential aspect of personal finance management. It empowers individuals to make informed financial decisions, set achievable goals, manage debt, and plan for a secure financial future. Regular evaluation and monitoring of financial health enable adjustments and improvements, leading to a more stable and prosperous financial life.

DEFINITION AND SCOPE OF PERSONAL FINANCE

Personal finance refers to the management of an individual's financial resources, decisions, and activities to achieve financial goals, secure financial well-being, and improve overall financial health. It encompasses the planning, budgeting, saving, investing, spending, insurance, and retirement planning that an individual engages in to attain their financial objectives.

The scope of personal finance is broad and includes various aspects related to managing one's money and financial affairs effectively. Key components of the scope of personal finance include:

1. **Financial Goal Setting**: Identifying and establishing short-term and long-term financial objectives, such as buying a house, funding education, starting a business, or planning for retirement.

2. **Budgeting and Spending**: Creating a budget to manage income and expenses, allocating funds for essential needs, discretionary spending, and savings, while ensuring financial stability and debt management.

3. **Savings and Investments**: Implementing strategies to save money and invest in various financial instruments like stocks, bonds, mutual funds, real estate, and other assets to grow wealth over time and achieve financial goals.

4. **Debt Management**: Understanding, monitoring, and managing debt responsibly, including strategies for debt reduction, consolidation, and smart borrowing.

5. **Insurance and Risk Management**: Evaluating and obtaining appropriate insurance coverage to mitigate financial risks associated with health, life, property, and liability, ensuring protection against unforeseen events.

6. **Retirement Planning**: Planning and saving for retirement by estimating retirement needs, contributing to retirement accounts (e.g., 401(k), IRA), and strategizing for post-retirement income and lifestyle.

7. **Tax Planning**: Optimizing tax efficiency by understanding tax laws, deductions, credits, and utilizing tax-saving investment options to reduce tax liabilities.

8. **Estate Planning and Wealth Transfer**: Strategically planning the distribution of assets and wealth to heirs and beneficiaries, considering legal and tax implications.

9. **Financial Literacy and Education**: Acquiring knowledge and understanding financial concepts, principles, and practices to make informed financial decisions and enhance financial literacy.

10. **Financial Behavior and Psychology**: Recognizing and addressing behavioral and psychological factors that influence financial decision-making and adopting healthy financial habits.

11. **Credit Management**: Understanding credit scores, credit reports, and credit usage, and maintaining good credit standing for favorable borrowing terms and financial stability.

The scope of personal finance continually evolves due to changes in economic conditions, advancements in financial technology, shifts in regulatory landscapes, and evolving lifestyles. It is essential for individuals to stay informed and adapt to the changing financial landscape to effectively manage their personal finances and achieve financial well-being.

HISTORICAL CONTEXT AND EVOLUTION OF PERSONAL FINANCE

The historical context and evolution of personal finance can be traced back to ancient civilizations where rudimentary forms of financial management and transactions were in practice. Over millennia, personal finance has evolved from simple barter systems to complex financial markets and digital banking. Here is an overview of the historical development and transformation of personal finance:

1. **Ancient Times and Barter System (Pre-3000 BC)**: In ancient civilizations, individuals engaged in a barter system, exchanging goods and services directly. There were no standardized forms of currency, and financial transactions were based on the mutual agreement of value between the parties involved.

2. **Metal Coins and Ancient Economies (Around 600 BC)**: The use of metal coins, such as gold, silver, and copper, emerged in various ancient civilizations like Lydia (modern-day Turkey), Greece, and China. The introduction of standardized currency facilitated trade and provided a more efficient medium for financial transactions.

3. **Early Banking and Moneylending (Middle Ages)**: During the Middle Ages, banking and moneylending began to take shape. Merchants and traders needed a secure place to store their money and valuables, leading to the establishment of early banks and lending practices.

4. **Renaissance and Modern Banking (15th-16th centuries)**: The Renaissance period marked a significant advancement in banking and finance. The Medici family in Florence, Italy, played a

pivotal role in modernizing banking, introducing double-entry accounting, and expanding the concept of banking beyond money storage to lending and investing.

5. **Industrial Revolution and Modern Finance (18th-19th centuries)**: The Industrial Revolution brought about economic and technological advancements, giving rise to modern financial institutions, stock exchanges, and the development of investment opportunities. Publicly traded companies emerged, attracting investors and creating wealth through stock ownership.

6. **Great Depression and Regulation (1930s)**: The Great Depression in the 1930s highlighted the need for financial regulation and consumer protection. Governments established regulatory bodies, such as the Securities and Exchange Commission (SEC) in the United States, to oversee financial markets and prevent another economic collapse.

7. **Post-World War II and Economic Growth (1940s-1960s)**: After World War II, economic growth and the rise of the middle class led to increased focus on personal financial planning. The concept of budgeting, saving, and investing for the future gained prominence during this period.

8. **Digital Age and Technological Revolution (Late 20th century)**: The advent of computers, the internet, and financial technology (fintech) in the late 20th century revolutionized personal finance. Online banking, investment platforms, budgeting apps, and financial education became easily accessible to the masses.

9. **Globalization and Diversification (Late 20th century to present)**: Globalization expanded investment opportunities, allowing individuals to diversify their portfolios beyond their domestic markets. Investment in international stocks, mutual funds, and other assets became more common.

10. **Personal Finance in the 21st Century (Present)**: In the 21st century, personal finance has evolved further with the rise of robo-advisors, cryptocurrencies, decentralized finance (DeFi), and a focus on financial literacy. Automation, AI-powered financial planning tools, and accessible online education have empowered individuals to manage their finances more efficiently.

In summary, personal finance has undergone significant evolution, driven by changes in society, technology, regulation, and economic structures. From basic barter systems to a sophisticated, interconnected global financial ecosystem, the journey of personal finance continues to adapt to the needs and advancements of modern society.

THE IMPORTANCE OF BEING FINANCIALLY LITERATE

Financial literacy is an essential skill that empowers individuals to make informed and effective financial decisions, leading to improved financial well-being and a higher quality of life. Here are several key reasons highlighting the importance of being financially literate:

1. **Sound Financial Decision-making**: Financial literacy equips individuals with the knowledge and skills to evaluate financial options critically. It helps in understanding the implications and outcomes of different decisions, enabling individuals to choose the best financial path aligned with their goals and circumstances.

2. **Budgeting and Spending Wisely**: Understanding personal finance allows individuals to create and adhere to a budget effectively. It helps in tracking income, managing expenses, prioritizing spending, and avoiding unnecessary debt, resulting in improved financial stability and disciplined financial behavior.

3. **Debt Management**: Financial literacy educates individuals on managing debt responsibly. It provides insights into types of debt, interest rates, repayment strategies, and the consequences of accumulating excessive debt. This knowledge empowers individuals to develop strategies to reduce and manage debt effectively.

4. **Saving and Investing for the Future**: Being financially literate enables individuals to comprehend the benefits of saving and investing. It helps in understanding various investment options, risk tolerance, diversification, and the power of compounding, allowing individuals to grow their wealth and plan for future financial goals.

5. **Risk Management and Insurance Understanding**: Financial literacy helps individuals understand the importance of insurance and risk management. Knowing the types of insurance, coverage options, and how insurance works allows individuals to protect themselves, their assets, and their families from unforeseen events and financial hardships.

6. **Retirement Planning**: Financial literacy provides the foundation for effective retirement planning. Understanding the significance of retirement savings, estimating retirement needs, selecting appropriate retirement accounts, and developing a retirement plan are crucial aspects of financial literacy to ensure a secure and comfortable retirement.

7. **Financial Resilience in Emergencies**: Being financially literate enables individuals to prepare for emergencies by creating an emergency fund. In unforeseen circumstances such as medical emergencies, job loss, or natural disasters, having savings and knowing how to manage finances in a crisis is vital for financial resilience.

8. **Improved Credit Management**: Financial literacy helps in understanding credit scores, credit reports, and their impact on financial well-being. With this knowledge, individuals can make

informed decisions to maintain a good credit standing, leading to favorable borrowing terms and financial stability.

9. **Empowerment and Confidence**: Financial literacy empowers individuals to take control of their financial future. The confidence gained from understanding financial concepts allows individuals to engage with financial professionals, ask pertinent questions, and advocate for their financial interests effectively.

10. **Breaking Cycles of Poverty and Debt**: By promoting financial literacy, we can break cycles of poverty and debt that often persist within families and communities. Educating individuals about financial principles helps in creating a positive impact on future generations, promoting economic stability and growth.

In conclusion, financial literacy is a fundamental life skill that can significantly enhance an individual's financial well-being, enabling them to navigate the complex financial landscape, achieve their goals, and build a secure and prosperous future. Governments, educational institutions, and organizations should continue to emphasize and promote financial education to ensure a financially literate society.

HOW FINANCIAL LITERACY EMPOWERS INDIVIDUALS TO MAKE INFORMED DECISIONS

Financial literacy is a powerful tool that empowers individuals to make informed and effective decisions regarding their finances. Here's how financial literacy provides this empowerment:

1. **Understanding Financial Concepts**: Financial literacy provides individuals with knowledge about fundamental financial concepts such as budgeting, saving, investing, debt management, taxes, and retirement planning. Understanding these concepts allows individuals to navigate financial decisions with confidence and clarity.

2. **Evaluating Options and Risks**: Being financially literate enables individuals to evaluate various financial options, such as different investment opportunities or types of insurance. They can assess the risks associated with each option and make informed decisions based on their risk tolerance and financial goals.

3. **Setting Realistic Financial Goals**: Financial literacy assists individuals in setting clear, achievable financial goals. By understanding their financial situation, they can set targets for saving, investing, debt reduction, and other aspects of their financial life. Realistic goals serve as a roadmap for their financial journey.

4. **Effective Budgeting and Spending**: Financial literacy equips individuals with the skills to create and manage a budget effectively. They can track their income and expenditures, allocate funds for essential needs, and control unnecessary spending. This enables them to achieve a balanced financial life.

5. **Smart Debt Management**: Individuals with financial literacy understand the implications of different types of debt, interest rates, and repayment strategies. This knowledge enables them to manage debt wisely, avoid accumulating excessive debt, and work toward paying off existing debt efficiently.

6. **Investment Decision-making**: Financial literacy allows individuals to understand various investment options, including stocks, bonds, mutual funds, and real estate. They can evaluate the potential returns, risks, and time horizons associated with each investment, aiding them in making sound investment decisions aligned with their financial goals.

7. **Tax Efficiency and Planning**: Knowledge of tax laws and financial literacy enables individuals to optimize their tax strategies. They can identify deductions, credits, and tax-advantaged

investment options, minimizing tax liabilities and retaining more of their income for savings and investments.

8. **Planning for Retirement**: Financial literacy is crucial for effective retirement planning. Individuals can estimate their retirement needs, calculate how much to save, choose appropriate retirement accounts, and develop a personalized retirement plan to ensure financial security during their retirement years.

9. **Financial Risk Mitigation**: Understanding financial concepts empowers individuals to recognize and mitigate financial risks effectively. This includes understanding the importance of insurance, emergency funds, and diversifying investments to protect against unexpected events and market fluctuations.

10. **Improving Credit Health**: Financial literacy helps individuals comprehend how their financial decisions impact their credit score and overall credit health. They can maintain good credit by paying bills on time, managing credit utilization, and understanding how credit scores influence borrowing terms.

11. **Confidence and Independence**: Ultimately, financial literacy provides individuals with the confidence and independence to make their own financial decisions. They can seek advice, but they are not solely reliant on others. This empowerment fosters a sense of control and responsibility over their financial well-being.

In conclusion, financial literacy is a catalyst for informed decision-making, enabling individuals to make choices that align with their financial goals, reduce financial stress, and pave the way for a secure financial future. It promotes financial independence and resilience, allowing individuals to navigate the complexities of the financial world with competence and confidence.

UNDERSTANDING FINANCIAL WELL-BEING AND ITS COMPONENTS

Financial well-being is a comprehensive and holistic state of being where an individual's financial resources and financial behaviors align with their values and needs, ultimately leading to a sense of financial security, stability, and contentment. It's not just about having a certain amount of money but encompasses how one manages, saves, invests, and uses their financial resources to support their overall well-being and life goals.

Components of Financial Well-being:

1. **Financial Security**: Financial security is a fundamental component of financial well-being. It involves having a stable and predictable financial situation, ensuring that basic needs like housing, food, healthcare, and education are adequately met. This component also includes having an emergency fund to cover unexpected expenses.

2. **Financial Stability**: Financial stability is the ability to maintain a consistent and sustainable financial situation over time. It involves having a steady income, managing expenses, and avoiding large fluctuations in one's financial position. Stability provides a sense of assurance and reduces financial stress.

3. **Financial Freedom and Flexibility**: Financial well-being allows individuals the freedom to make choices about their lives without being constrained by financial limitations. It provides the flexibility to pursue personal goals, whether it's starting a business, traveling, further education, or other aspirations, without financial barriers.

4. **Financial Independence**: Financial independence signifies the ability to sustain one's lifestyle and cover expenses without being reliant on external financial support. Achieving financial

independence involves prudent financial planning, saving, investing, and smart financial decisions.

5. **Debt Management**: Effective debt management is an essential component of financial well-being. It involves understanding, minimizing, and managing debt responsibly, ensuring that debt levels are manageable and not overwhelming, and formulating strategies for debt repayment.

6. **Savings and Investments**: The component of savings and investments involves setting aside a portion of income for the future, whether it's short-term savings for emergencies or long-term investments for retirement. Effective saving and investing help in building wealth, securing financial goals, and generating passive income.

7. **Financial Literacy and Education**: Understanding financial concepts and having the necessary knowledge to make informed financial decisions is crucial for financial well-being. Financial literacy empowers individuals to navigate complex financial landscapes, manage finances wisely, and make sound financial choices.

8. **Retirement Planning**: Retirement planning is a vital component, ensuring that individuals are financially prepared for their retirement years. It involves estimating retirement needs, contributing to retirement accounts, and developing a strategy to maintain the desired lifestyle post-retirement.

9. **Economic and Social Well-being**: Financial well-being is also closely linked to broader aspects of well-being, such as access to quality healthcare, education, community engagement, and a sense of belonging. Economic and social well-being contribute to an individual's overall satisfaction and contentment with their financial situation.

10. **Health and Well-being**: Physical and mental health are significant components of overall well-being, and they are intertwined with financial well-being. Financial stability and security positively impact an individual's ability to afford healthcare, maintain a healthy lifestyle, and reduce stress.

In summary, financial well-being is a multidimensional concept that encompasses various aspects of an individual's financial life and overall quality of life. Achieving financial well-being involves striking a balance among financial security, stability, freedom, and fulfilling personal goals and needs.

HOW FINANCIAL WELL-BEING IMPACTS OVERALL QUALITY OF LIFE

Financial well-being significantly impacts an individual's overall quality of life in several ways, ranging from meeting basic needs to achieving life goals and fostering emotional well-being. Here are the ways in which financial well-being influences an individual's overall quality of life:

1. **Meeting Basic Needs**: Financial well-being ensures that an individual can meet their basic needs, including food, shelter, healthcare, education, and utilities. Having the financial capacity to provide for these essentials directly contributes to an improved quality of life.

2. **Reducing Stress and Anxiety**: Financial stability and security reduce stress and anxiety associated with financial challenges. When individuals are financially secure and have a safety net, they can face life's uncertainties with confidence, leading to improved mental and emotional well-being.

3. **Improving Physical Health**: Financial well-being positively impacts physical health by providing access to better healthcare, nutritious food, fitness facilities, and stress-reduction activities. Financially secure individuals can afford regular check-ups and medical treatments, enhancing their overall health and longevity.

4. **Enhancing Mental Health**: Financial well-being is linked to better mental health outcomes. Individuals who are financially stable experience reduced anxiety and depression, allowing them to maintain a more positive outlook and cope better with life's challenges.

5. **Enabling Educational Opportunities**: Financial well-being allows individuals to invest in education, whether for themselves or their children. Access to quality education opens up opportunities for personal growth, better career prospects, and higher earning potential, contributing to an enhanced quality of life.

6. **Fulfilling Personal Aspirations and Hobbies**: Financial well-being enables individuals to pursue their passions, hobbies, and interests, whether it's traveling, sports, arts, or cultural experiences. Having the financial means to engage in activities that bring joy and fulfillment enriches their overall quality of life.

7. **Strengthening Relationships and Social Connections**: Financial stability fosters healthy relationships and social interactions. Individuals can invest time and resources in building and maintaining meaningful relationships with family and friends, leading to a more fulfilling and enriched social life.

8. **Promoting Long-Term Security and Peace of Mind**: Financial well-being allows for long-term planning and financial security, especially during retirement. Knowing that one has saved and invested enough for a comfortable retirement provides peace of mind and a sense of security, enhancing the overall quality of life in the later years.

9. **Supporting Civic and Community Involvement**: Financial well-being enables individuals to contribute to their communities, charities, or causes they believe in. Being financially stable allows them to give back and make a positive impact on society, which adds to their sense of purpose and overall life satisfaction.

10. **Empowering Life Choices and Decision-making**: Financial well-being provides individuals with the freedom to make choices aligned with their values and goals. They can make decisions about their careers, homes, lifestyles, and investments, which reflect their aspirations, preferences, and priorities, thus enhancing their overall life satisfaction.

In conclusion, financial well-being is deeply intertwined with an individual's overall quality of life. It impacts physical and mental health, supports personal and professional growth, nurtures relationships, and enables the pursuit of a fulfilling and purposeful life. Achieving financial well-being is a critical step toward enhancing one's holistic well-being and living a satisfying life.

SUPPLY AND DEMAND

Supply and demand are fundamental economic concepts that describe the relationship between the quantity of a good or service that producers are willing to provide and the quantity that consumers are willing to purchase at a given price in a particular market. These concepts play a crucial role in determining market equilibrium, prices, and overall economic behavior.

1. **Supply**: Supply refers to the quantity of a good or service that producers or suppliers are willing and able to offer for sale in a given market during a specific time period. Supply is influenced by factors such as production costs, technology, government policies, and the number of suppliers in the market. Generally, the higher the price of a good, the more producers are willing to supply, ceteris paribus (all other things being equal).

2. **Demand**: Demand represents the quantity of a good or service that consumers are willing and able to purchase at various prices during a specific time period. Demand is influenced by factors like consumer preferences, income, population, advertising, and the prices of substitute or complementary goods. Typically, as the price of a good decreases, the quantity demanded increases, assuming other factors remain constant.

3. **Law of Demand**: The Law of Demand states that, all else being equal, there is an inverse relationship between the price of a good and the quantity demanded of that good. In simpler terms, when the price of a good rises, the quantity demanded decreases, and vice versa.

4. **Law of Supply**: The Law of Supply asserts that, all else being equal, there is a direct relationship between the price of a good and the quantity supplied of that good. In other words, as the price of a good increases, the quantity supplied by producers also increases.

5. **Equilibrium**: Equilibrium in a market occurs at the point where the quantity demanded equals the quantity supplied. This is the market-clearing price, and it's the price at which both buyers and sellers are satisfied. If the price is below this equilibrium, there is excess demand (a shortage), and if it's above, there is excess supply (a surplus).

6. **Shifts in Supply and Demand Curves**: Changes in factors other than price that influence supply or demand cause the entire supply or demand curve to shift. An increase in supply shifts the supply curve to the right, leading to lower prices and higher quantity. Conversely, an increase in demand shifts the demand curve to the right, resulting in higher prices and a higher quantity.

Understanding supply and demand dynamics is vital for businesses, policymakers, and consumers. It helps businesses plan production and pricing strategies, governments design effective economic policies, and consumers make informed purchasing decisions. The interaction between supply and demand is central to market economies and determines the allocation of resources and prices of goods and services.

INFLATION, DEFLATION, AND THEIR EFFECTS ON PERSONAL FINANCES

Inflation and deflation are two contrasting economic phenomena that have significant impacts on the purchasing power of money and, consequently, on an individual's personal finances. Understanding these concepts and their effects is crucial for financial planning and decision-making.

1. **Inflation**: Inflation is a sustained increase in the general level of prices for goods and services in an economy over a period of time, resulting in a decrease in the purchasing power of money. Inflation erodes the value of money, meaning that over time, the same amount of money will buy fewer goods and services.

Effects on Personal Finances:

- **Purchasing Power Reduction**: Inflation diminishes the purchasing power of your money. What you could buy for $100 last year might cost $110 this year due to inflation.

- **Impact on Savings**: Inflation erodes the real value of savings held in cash or low-yield assets. If the rate of inflation is higher than the return on your investments, your purchasing power decreases.

- **Interest Rates and Loans**: Central banks often raise interest rates to combat inflation. This can lead to higher borrowing costs for mortgages, auto loans, and other debts, impacting your budget and financial planning.

- **Cost of Living**: Inflation generally results in an increased cost of living, affecting daily expenses like groceries, utilities, rent, and healthcare. It can strain household budgets and require adjustments in spending habits.

2. **Deflation**: Deflation is the sustained decrease in the general price level of goods and services, leading to an increase in the purchasing power of money. While this might seem beneficial, deflation can also have adverse effects on the economy and personal finances.

Effects on Personal Finances:

- **Increased Purchasing Power**: In deflation, your money's purchasing power increases. Goods and services become cheaper, allowing you to buy more with the same amount of money.

- **Debt Burden**: While your purchasing power increases, if you have debts, deflation can make it harder to repay them. The real value of your debt increases, and this can lead to financial strain.

- **Delayed Spending**: Deflation may encourage consumers to delay spending, anticipating lower prices in the future. While this might be beneficial for consumers, it can hinder economic growth.

Both inflation and deflation can have significant implications for an individual's financial situation. Balancing the effects of these economic phenomena requires prudent financial planning, diversifying investments, considering the rate of inflation while setting financial goals, and monitoring changes in the economic environment. It's important to adjust financial strategies accordingly to mitigate the impact of these economic fluctuations on personal finances.

SHORT-TERM VS. LONG-TERM FINANCIAL DECISIONS

Short-term and long-term financial decisions are distinguished by the time horizon over which they impact an individual's financial situation and objectives. Each type of decision serves different purposes and has distinct implications for an individual's financial well-being.

1. **Short-Term Financial Decisions**:

Short-term financial decisions pertain to choices that affect an individual's finances in the near future, typically within the next year or less. These decisions are immediate and focus on addressing current needs, managing day-to-day expenses, and handling short-term financial goals.

- **Budgeting and Spending**: Creating a budget to manage monthly income and expenses is a short-term financial decision. It involves allocating funds for immediate needs, such as rent, groceries, utilities, and discretionary spending.

- **Emergency Fund Management**: Establishing and maintaining an emergency fund to cover unexpected expenses like medical emergencies or car repairs is a short-term decision that provides financial security in the near future.

- **Debt Repayment Strategies**: Deciding on how to allocate funds to pay off short-term debts like credit card balances or personal loans within a few months is a short-term financial decision.

- **Cash Flow Management**: Ensuring there is enough liquidity to meet short-term obligations, including paying bills, mortgage, and other financial commitments, is crucial for short-term financial stability.

- **Investment in Short-Term Instruments**: Decisions to invest in low-risk, short-term instruments like certificates of deposit (CDs) or money market accounts to preserve capital or earn a small return in the short term.

2. **Long-Term Financial Decisions**:

Long-term financial decisions encompass choices that have a lasting impact on an individual's financial situation, often spanning many years or even decades. These decisions focus on achieving significant financial goals and ensuring a secure financial future.

- **Retirement Planning**: Making decisions and contributions to retirement accounts (e.g., 401(k), IRA) for long-term financial security during retirement is a critical long-term financial decision.

- **Investment Portfolio Strategy**: Developing a diversified investment portfolio aligned with long-term financial goals and risk tolerance to achieve capital growth and wealth accumulation over time.

- **Real Estate Investments**: Purchasing a home or investment property, which is a long-term financial decision that may appreciate in value and serve as a valuable asset.

- **Education Planning**: Planning and saving for a child's education or furthering one's own education by making decisions on savings plans or investment vehicles.

- **Estate and Legacy Planning**: Establishing an estate plan, creating trusts, and determining the distribution of assets to heirs and charitable organizations upon death are long-term financial decisions that ensure financial security for future generations.

- **Insurance and Retirement Products**: Acquiring life insurance, disability insurance, or annuities to provide financial protection and income during retirement are long-term decisions that offer financial security in the future.

In summary, short-term financial decisions revolve around immediate needs and goals, aiming to maintain financial stability in the present. On the other hand, long-term financial decisions are geared towards securing one's financial future, achieving significant life goals, and building financial resilience over an extended period. Both types of decisions are crucial for a well-rounded financial strategy and must be aligned with an individual's overall financial plan.

CONSEQUENCES OF FINANCIAL DECISIONS ON FUTURE GOALS AND LIFESTYLE

Financial decisions have a profound and lasting impact on an individual's future goals and lifestyle. The choices made today can significantly influence financial security, opportunities, and overall well-being in the years to come. Here are the potential consequences of financial decisions on future goals and lifestyle:

1. **Financial Security and Stability**:

   - **Savings and Investments**: Prudent decisions to save and invest can lead to financial security in the future, providing a safety net for emergencies, retirement, and other financial needs.

   - **Debt Management**: Responsible handling of debt helps maintain a healthy credit score and ensures that debt does not become an overwhelming burden, contributing to long-term financial stability.

2. **Ability to Achieve Goals**:

   - **Education Funding**: Planning and saving for education can enable individuals or their children to pursue higher education and achieve their career aspirations without being constrained by financial limitations.

   - **Homeownership**: Making well-informed decisions regarding homeownership allows for stability, potential equity growth, and a place to call home, contributing to a desired lifestyle and future financial stability.

3. **Retirement Preparedness**:

   - **Retirement Savings**: Prudent decisions to consistently save and invest for retirement ensure a comfortable and financially secure lifestyle during the retirement years.

- **Retirement Age and Lifestyle Choices**: Early retirement or a specific retirement lifestyle can be achieved through thoughtful financial planning and saving.

4. **Quality of Life and Opportunities**:

   - **Career and Skill Development**: Investments in education and skill development can lead to higher-paying job opportunities and a higher quality of life.

   - **Travel and Leisure**: Smart financial decisions allow for opportunities to travel and engage in leisure activities, enhancing one's overall quality of life.

5. **Legacy and Estate Planning**:

   - **Estate Distribution**: Thoughtful estate planning ensures that assets are distributed as per an individual's wishes, benefiting heirs and supporting future generations.

   - **Charitable Contributions**: Financial decisions to contribute to charitable causes allow for a positive impact on society and leave a meaningful legacy.

6. **Financial Freedom and Independence**:

   - **Early Retirement**: Effective financial planning and investment decisions can lead to the possibility of retiring early and enjoying financial independence at an earlier stage in life.

   - **Entrepreneurship and Business Ventures**: Decisions to invest in and start businesses can result in financial independence and the opportunity to shape one's career and lifestyle.

7. **Health and Well-being**:

- **Healthcare Expenses**: Financial decisions related to health insurance and saving for medical expenses influence the ability to access quality healthcare and maintain good health, impacting overall well-being.

8. **Creditworthiness and Borrowing Capacity**:

   - **Credit Score and Loan Terms**: Responsible financial decisions affect credit scores, impacting future borrowing capacity and the terms of loans for significant life purchases like homes or vehicles.

In conclusion, financial decisions are the cornerstone of an individual's future financial well-being and lifestyle. They can either pave the way for achieving goals, providing security, and enhancing one's quality of life or create financial challenges that hinder progress and limit opportunities. Making informed, strategic, and disciplined financial choices is vital for realizing future aspirations and leading a fulfilling life.

CREATING A PERSONAL BUDGET

Creating a personal budget is a fundamental step in managing finances effectively and achieving financial goals. A budget helps track income, plan expenses, save for the future, and control spending. Here's a step-by-step guide to creating a personal budget:

1. **Determine Income**: Begin by calculating your total monthly income. Include all sources of income, such as salary, freelance work, rental income, investments, etc. Use your after-tax income for accuracy.

2. **List Fixed Expenses**: Identify and list your fixed or essential monthly expenses, which remain relatively constant. These may include:

   - Rent or mortgage payments

- Utilities (electricity, water, gas)

- Insurance premiums (health, life, auto, home)

- Loan payments (car, student loans)

- Internet and phone bills

- Transportation (public transit, fuel)

3. **Account for Variable Expenses**: Record your variable or discretionary expenses, which can fluctuate monthly. Examples include:

- Groceries and dining out

- Entertainment (movies, concerts, hobbies)

- Clothing and personal care

- Gifts and donations

- Travel and vacations

- Miscellaneous expenses

4. **Factor in Savings and Investments**: Allocate a portion of your income towards savings, investments, and debt repayment. Set aside money for:

- Emergency fund

- Retirement contributions

- Debt repayment (credit cards, loans)

- Investments (stocks, bonds, retirement accounts)

5. **Calculate Total Expenses**: Add up your fixed and variable expenses, as well as savings and debt repayments, to determine your total monthly expenses.

6. **Compute the Difference (Income - Expenses)**: Subtract your total expenses from your total income to calculate the difference. A positive difference indicates a surplus, while a negative difference suggests a deficit.

7. **Adjust and Fine-Tune the Budget**:

   - If you have a surplus, consider allocating the excess to savings, investments, or paying down debt faster.

   - If you have a deficit, reevaluate your expenses and look for areas where you can cut back or reduce spending.

8. **Track and Monitor Expenses**:

   - Keep track of all your expenses by saving receipts or using budgeting apps. Categorize expenditures to understand where your money is going.

   - Regularly review your budget to ensure you're staying on track and making necessary adjustments as circumstances change.

9. **Stick to the Budget**:

   - Adhere to the budget by following the planned allocations for each expense category. Avoid overspending in one category at the expense of another.

   - Exercise discipline and stay committed to achieving your financial goals through the budget.

10. **Periodic Review and Adjustment**:

- Periodically review your budget (e.g., monthly or quarterly) to assess your financial progress and make adjustments based on changes in income, expenses, or financial goals.

Creating a personal budget is an ongoing process that requires dedication and flexibility. By managing your finances effectively through budgeting, you can work towards achieving your financial objectives and attaining financial stability.

TRACKING INCOME AND EXPENSES

Tracking income and expenses is a critical component of effective financial management. It provides a clear picture of where your money is coming from, how it is being spent, and helps in making informed financial decisions. Here's a step-by-step guide on how to track your income and expenses:

1. **Gather Income Information**: Start by gathering information about all your sources of income. This includes your salary, rental income, business income, dividends, interest, and any other sources of money you receive regularly.

2. **Categorize Income**: Organize your income into categories to clearly understand its sources and nature. Common categories may include:

   - Salary/Wages

   - Business Income

   - Rental Income

   - Investment Income

   - Miscellaneous Income

3. **Record Income Regularly**: Keep a record of all your income, noting the source, amount, and date of receipt. You can use a spreadsheet, a budgeting app, or simply a notebook for this purpose.

4. **List Your Expenses**: Create categories for your expenses to organize them effectively. Common expense categories include:

   - Housing (rent/mortgage, utilities)

   - Transportation (fuel, public transit, car maintenance)

   - Food (groceries, dining out)

   - Debt Payments (credit cards, loans)

   - Insurance (health, car, home)

   - Entertainment

   - Savings and Investments

5. **Record Expenses Daily or Regularly**: Make it a habit to record your expenses daily or regularly. Every time you spend money, note down the amount, category, and purpose of the expense.

6. **Use Technology for Tracking**: Consider using budgeting apps or financial software that can automatically track and categorize your expenses. These tools often link to your bank accounts and credit cards, making it easier to monitor your spending.

7. **Monitor and Review Regularly**: Periodically review your income and expenses. Check for any discrepancies, overspending, or areas where you can cut back. This review can help you adjust your budget and make better financial decisions.

8. **Analyze and Adjust**: Analyze your spending patterns to understand where your money is going. Identify areas where you can save or reallocate funds to meet financial goals. Adjust your budget accordingly.

9. **Set Budget Limits**: Establish budget limits for each expense category based on your income and financial goals. Stick to these limits to maintain financial discipline.

10. **Save Receipts and Invoices**: Keep receipts, invoices, and bills as proof of your expenses. This documentation will be helpful during tax time and for verifying your spending.

11. **Track Trends and Patterns**: Over time, observe spending trends and patterns. This will help you anticipate seasonal changes in expenses and plan accordingly.

12. **Educate Yourself and Seek Advice**: Learn about personal finance, budgeting, and ways to manage your money effectively. Consider consulting a financial advisor for personalized guidance.

By diligently tracking your income and expenses, you gain a clearer understanding of your financial habits and patterns. This knowledge allows you to make informed decisions, control your spending, save more, and work towards achieving your financial goals.

BUDGETING TOOLS AND SOFTWARE

Budgeting tools and software are essential resources that can help you manage your finances effectively, track income and expenses, set financial goals, and make informed financial decisions. Here are some popular budgeting tools and software:

1. **1. Mint**:

    - **Features**:

- Aggregates all financial accounts in one place.

- Tracks expenses and income.

- Creates budgets and provides personalized financial insights.

- Sends alerts for bill payments and unusual account activity.

- **Availability**: Web-based, iOS, Android.

2. **YNAB (You Need A Budget)**:

- **Features**:

  - Uses a zero-based budgeting approach.

  - Assigns every dollar to a specific category.

  - Helps users break the paycheck-to-paycheck cycle.

  - Offers educational resources and support.

- **Availability**: Web-based, iOS, Android.

3. **EveryDollar**:

- **Features**:

  - Follows a zero-based budgeting method.

  - Allows customization of spending categories.

  - Provides budget progress tracking.

  - Offers a free version with limited features and a paid version with more features.

- **Availability**: Web-based, iOS, Android.

4. **PocketGuard**:

   - **Features**:

     - Automatically tracks and categorizes expenses.

     - Shows an overview of finances and remaining funds.

     - Helps set spending limits for different categories.

     - Provides insights into spending patterns.

   - **Availability**: Web-based, iOS, Android.

5. **Personal Capital**:

   - **Features**:

     - Tracks investments, assets, and liabilities in addition to budgeting.

     - Offers retirement planning and investment management tools.

     - Provides a holistic view of your financial picture.

   - **Availability**: Web-based, iOS, Android.

6. **GoodBudget**:

   - **Features**:

     - Uses the envelope budgeting system.

     - Allows for sharing and syncing budgets with family members.

     - Provides expense tracking and reports.

- **Availability**: Web-based, iOS, Android.

7. **Tiller Money**:

   - **Features**:

     - Automates budget tracking in spreadsheets (e.g., Google Sheets, Excel).

     - Categorizes transactions and updates the budget daily.

     - Allows customization and flexibility using familiar spreadsheet interfaces.

   - **Availability**: Web-based.

8. **Simple**:

   - **Features**:

     - Provides a digital bank account with budgeting tools.

     - Categorizes transactions automatically.

     - Allows setting financial goals.

   - **Availability**: Web-based, iOS, Android.

9. **Wally**:

   - **Features**:

     - Tracks expenses, income, and savings goals.

     - Offers a clean and intuitive user interface.

     - Supports multiple currencies and offers insights into spending patterns.

   - **Availability**: iOS, Android.

10. **Honeydue**:

- **Features**:

    - Designed for couples to manage finances together.

    - Allows tracking joint and individual expenses.

    - Provides bill reminders and real-time transaction tracking.

- **Availability**: iOS, Android.

Choose a budgeting tool or software that aligns with your financial goals, preferences, and ease of use. Regularly using a budgeting tool can significantly improve your financial awareness and help you achieve your financial objectives.

TYPES OF DEBT AND THEIR IMPACT

Debt is a financial obligation that arises when one party borrows money from another and agrees to repay it with interest over time. Debt can be classified into various types based on different criteria, such as interest rates, repayment terms, and purpose. Each type of debt has its own characteristics and impacts on an individual's financial situation. Here are some common types of debt and their impacts:

1. **Consumer Debt**:

- **Description**: Consumer debt is debt incurred for personal consumption rather than investment. It includes credit card debt, auto loans, and personal loans.

- **Impact**:

    - High-interest rates on credit card debt can lead to significant financial burden and increase the overall cost of purchases.

- Excessive consumer debt can strain a person's budget, limit savings, and hinder progress toward financial goals.

2. **Mortgage Debt**:

- **Description**: Mortgage debt is a loan secured by real estate, typically used to purchase a home or property.

- **Impact**:

  - Homeownership builds equity and potentially appreciates in value over time, leading to potential wealth accumulation.

  - However, failure to repay a mortgage can result in foreclosure and the loss of the property.

3. **Student Loans**:

- **Description**: Student loans are taken to fund education expenses and are typically repaid after completing education or dropping below half-time enrollment.

- **Impact**:

  - Student loans can provide access to higher education, improving future earning potential and career opportunities.

  - However, excessive student loan debt can lead to financial strain and delay other life milestones like homeownership or starting a family.

4. **Auto Loans**:

- **Description**: Auto loans are loans used to finance the purchase of a vehicle.

- **Impact**:

  - Auto loans allow access to transportation and can improve mobility and job opportunities.

  - High-interest rates or long loan terms can increase the overall cost of the vehicle and strain the borrower's budget.

5. **Personal Loans**:

   - **Description**: Personal loans are unsecured loans provided by banks, credit unions, or online lenders, typically used for various personal purposes.

   - **Impact**:

     - Personal loans can be used to consolidate debt, cover unexpected expenses, or finance home improvements.

     - High-interest rates and fees can increase the cost of borrowing and affect the borrower's financial stability.

6. **Payday Loans and Cash Advances**:

   - **Description**: Payday loans are short-term, high-interest loans often used by individuals facing immediate financial needs, usually to be repaid by the next paycheck.

   - **Impact**:

     - High-interest rates and fees make payday loans very expensive and can trap borrowers in a cycle of debt.

     - Borrowers may find it difficult to break free from the debt cycle and meet ongoing financial obligations.

7. **Business Loans**:

- **Description**: Business loans are debt arrangements taken by entrepreneurs to fund and operate their businesses.

- **Impact**:

  - Business loans can provide necessary capital for growth, expansion, or operational needs, enhancing business viability and profitability.

  - However, business debt carries risks, and failure to repay can lead to financial strain and business failure.

Understanding the types of debt and their impacts is crucial for making informed financial decisions. It's important to manage debt wisely, choose debt with favorable terms, and repay debt in a timely manner to minimize adverse effects on personal finances and achieve long-term financial well-being.

STRATEGIES FOR DEBT MANAGEMENT

Effectively managing debt is essential for maintaining financial stability and working towards financial goals. Here are several strategies for managing debt:

1. **Create a Comprehensive List of Debts**:

   - List all your debts, including the type of debt, outstanding balance, interest rates, minimum payments, and due dates. Having a clear overview will help prioritize and strategize repayment.

2. **Prioritize Repayment**:

- Rank your debts based on interest rates or the debt with the smallest balance (debt snowball method). Focus on paying off high-interest debts first to save money on interest or smaller debts for a sense of achievement and motivation.

3. **Develop a Budget**:

   - Create a realistic budget that includes all your income and expenses. Allocate a portion of your income to debt repayment while ensuring you cover all necessary living expenses and savings.

4. **Negotiate Interest Rates**:

   - Contact your creditors to negotiate lower interest rates, especially if you have a good payment history. Lower rates can significantly reduce the total amount you repay over time.

5. **Consolidate Debts**:

   - Consider consolidating multiple debts into a single loan with a lower interest rate. This simplifies payments and may reduce your overall interest burden.

6. **Refinance Loans**:

   - If applicable, consider refinancing loans like student loans, mortgages, or auto loans to secure lower interest rates and more favorable terms, reducing monthly payments and overall costs.

7. **Employ the Debt Avalanche Method**:

- Allocate extra funds towards the debt with the highest interest rate while paying the minimum on others. Once the highest-interest debt is paid, move to the next highest, and so on.

8. **Use Windfalls Wisely**:

- Utilize any unexpected financial gains (tax refunds, bonuses, gifts) to make lump sum debt payments. This accelerates debt repayment and reduces the overall interest paid.

9. **Avoid Taking on New Debt**:

- Stop adding to your debt load. Cut down on credit card usage and avoid taking out new loans unless absolutely necessary.

10. **Seek Professional Advice**:

- Consult a credit counselor or financial advisor to create a personalized debt management plan. They can provide strategies, negotiate with creditors, and offer guidance to help you regain control over your finances.

11. **Build an Emergency Fund**:

- Set aside a small portion of your income each month to build an emergency fund. Having savings can prevent relying on credit for unexpected expenses.

12. **Educate Yourself About Financial Literacy**:

- Improve your financial knowledge and skills to make informed decisions regarding debt, spending, and investment. Understanding personal finance helps in avoiding debt traps and managing debt effectively.

13. **Stay Committed and Patient**:

- Managing debt is a long-term commitment. Stay patient, dedicated, and persistent in your efforts to reduce debt and work towards a debt-free future.

Remember, the key to successful debt management is discipline, a clear plan, and consistent efforts to repay debt while also maintaining a sustainable lifestyle. Tailor these strategies to your specific financial situation and goals.

DEBT REPAYMENT PLANS

Debt repayment plans outline structured approaches to pay off debts systematically, efficiently, and ultimately achieve financial freedom. Here are several common debt repayment plans you can consider based on your financial situation and preferences:

1. **Debt Snowball Method**:

   - **Process**: List your debts from the smallest balance to the largest, regardless of interest rates. Allocate extra funds to pay off the smallest debt first while making minimum payments on other debts. Once the smallest debt is paid off, use those payments for the next smallest debt, creating a "snowball" effect.

   - **Advantages**: Provides psychological motivation by achieving quick wins, boosting morale to tackle larger debts.

2. **Debt Avalanche Method**:

   - **Process**: List your debts from the highest interest rate to the lowest. Allocate extra funds to pay off the debt with the highest interest rate first while making minimum payments on other debts. After paying off the highest interest debt, move to the next highest, creating a cascading effect.

- **Advantages**: Saves the most money on interest payments over the long term.

3. **Debt Consolidation**:

   - **Process**: Combine multiple debts into a single debt with a lower interest rate. This can be done through a debt consolidation loan, balance transfer credit card, or home equity loan.

   - **Advantages**: Simplifies payments and may reduce overall interest payments, making it easier to manage and repay debt.

4. **Debt Management Plan (DMP)**:

   - **Process**: Work with a credit counseling agency to negotiate lower interest rates, waive fees, and create a structured repayment plan. You make a single monthly payment to the agency, and they distribute it to your creditors.

   - **Advantages**: Provides professional assistance and guidance to help manage and repay debt effectively.

5. **Bi-Weekly Payments**:

   - **Process**: Instead of making monthly payments, make half of your monthly payment every two weeks. This results in 26 half-payments or 13 full payments per year, effectively making an extra payment annually.

   - **Advantages**: Helps pay off debt faster, saving on interest over the loan term.

6. **Debt Settlement**:

- **Process**: Negotiate with creditors to settle your debt for less than the full amount owed. Typically, a lump sum payment is made to clear the debt, and the remaining balance is forgiven.

- **Advantages**: Can significantly reduce the total amount owed, but may impact your credit score and may have tax implications.

7. **Income-Driven Repayment (IDR) Plan for Student Loans**:

- **Process**: Tailors your student loan payments based on your income and family size. Payments can be as low as zero if your income is very low.

- **Advantages**: Helps manage student loan payments based on your financial capacity, especially for federal student loans.

8. **Rollover Method**:

- **Process**: Once you pay off a debt, take the amount you were paying on that debt and apply it to the next debt, creating a rolling effect.

- **Advantages**: Maximizes debt repayment momentum and accelerates the overall debt payoff process.

Choose a debt repayment plan that aligns with your financial situation, preferences, and goals. It's important to remain disciplined, consistent, and committed to your chosen plan to successfully reduce and eliminate your debts. Additionally, seeking guidance from a financial advisor or counselor can provide valuable insights and support in developing a suitable repayment strategy.

IMPORTANCE OF SAVINGS AND EMERGENCY FUNDS

Savings and emergency funds are crucial components of sound financial planning, providing financial security, stability, and a safety net to individuals and households. Here's a detailed explanation of their importance:

1. **Financial Security**:

   - **Savings**: Accumulating savings over time creates a financial cushion that protects you from unexpected expenses, job loss, or economic downturns. It gives you the confidence that you can weather financial challenges without relying heavily on credit or loans.

   - **Emergency Fund**: An emergency fund offers immediate financial security to cover unforeseen expenses like medical emergencies, car repairs, or urgent home repairs, preventing you from going into debt to meet these needs.

2. **Financial Independence and Peace of Mind**:

   - **Savings**: Having savings provides a sense of financial independence, reducing stress and anxiety related to money matters. It allows you to pursue opportunities, invest, or take risks that can improve your financial well-being.

   - **Emergency Fund**: An emergency fund gives you peace of mind knowing that you have a safety net to fall back on in case of unexpected events, allowing you to navigate life's uncertainties with confidence.

3. **Debt Prevention and Management**:

   - **Savings**: By having savings, you can avoid resorting to high-interest loans or credit cards to cover unexpected expenses, reducing your dependency on debt.

- **Emergency Fund**: An emergency fund helps prevent the accumulation of debt during financial emergencies, ensuring that you remain on track with your debt repayment plans.

4. **Opportunity for Investments and Growth**:

   - **Savings**: Savings provide a pool of funds that can be used for investments, helping you grow your wealth over time through various investment avenues.

   - **Emergency Fund**: An emergency fund allows you to invest the rest of your savings without constantly worrying about unexpected expenses, facilitating strategic investment planning.

5. **Financial Flexibility and Adaptability**:

   - **Savings**: Having savings offers the flexibility to make lifestyle changes, pursue education, or start a business, as you have a financial foundation to support your choices.

   - **Emergency Fund**: An emergency fund allows you to quickly adapt to unforeseen circumstances, providing the flexibility to handle unexpected financial needs or opportunities that may arise.

6. **Long-Term Financial Goals Achievement**:

   - **Savings**: Savings help you achieve long-term goals such as homeownership, education, retirement, or travel by accumulating funds gradually and consistently.

   - **Emergency Fund**: An emergency fund safeguards your long-term financial goals by preventing setbacks due to unexpected expenses, ensuring you stay on course to achieve your objectives.

7. **Reduced Stress and Improved Well-being**:

- **Savings**: Having savings reduces financial stress, promoting overall well-being, better mental health, and improved relationships due to reduced financial strain.

- **Emergency Fund**: An emergency fund alleviates anxiety related to financial emergencies, allowing you to focus on your personal and professional growth.

In conclusion, both savings and emergency funds are vital for building a secure financial future, managing financial emergencies, and achieving long-term financial goals. It's essential to prioritize and consistently contribute to both to enhance financial stability and well-being.

TYPES OF INVESTMENTS (STOCKS, BONDS, MUTUAL FUNDS)

Investing is a crucial part of financial planning and wealth-building. Various types of investments are available, each with its own characteristics, risk levels, and potential returns. Here are the most common types of investments:

1. **Stocks**:

- **Description**: Stocks represent ownership shares in a company. When you buy a stock, you become a partial owner of the company and share in its profits and losses.

- **Risk and Return**: Stocks have higher potential returns but also higher risk due to market volatility. Prices can fluctuate rapidly based on company performance, economic factors, and market sentiment.

2. **Bonds**:

- **Description**: Bonds are debt securities issued by governments, municipalities, or corporations. When you buy a bond, you are essentially lending money to the issuer in exchange for periodic interest payments and the return of the principal at maturity.

- **Risk and Return**: Bonds are generally considered lower risk compared to stocks but offer lower potential returns. The risk varies based on the issuer's creditworthiness and the bond's terms.

3. **Mutual Funds**:

- **Description**: Mutual funds pool money from multiple investors to invest in a diversified portfolio of stocks, bonds, or other securities managed by a professional fund manager.

- **Risk and Return**: Mutual funds offer diversification, spreading risk across multiple assets. The risk and potential return depend on the fund's investment objective and the underlying assets.

4. **Exchange-Traded Funds (ETFs)**:

- **Description**: ETFs are similar to mutual funds but are traded on stock exchanges like individual stocks. They typically track an index, sector, commodity, or asset class.

- **Risk and Return**: ETFs provide diversification like mutual funds and are traded throughout the day. They often have lower fees and can offer returns based on the performance of the underlying assets.

5. **Real Estate Investment Trusts (REITs)**:

- **Description**: REITs are companies that own, operate, or finance real estate that produces income. They allow investors to invest in real estate without directly owning physical properties.

- **Risk and Return**: REITs offer potential for regular income through dividends and capital appreciation. The risk and return vary based on the type of real estate and market conditions.

6. **Certificates of Deposit (CDs)**:

- **Description**: CDs are time deposits offered by banks with fixed terms (e.g., 3 months to 5 years). Investors deposit a fixed amount and receive interest upon maturity.

- **Risk and Return**: CDs are low-risk investments with a predictable, fixed interest rate. However, the returns are typically lower compared to other investments.

7. **Savings Accounts and Money Market Accounts**:

- **Description**: These are interest-bearing accounts offered by banks and credit unions where you can deposit and withdraw funds, usually with limited transactions.

- **Risk and Return**: Savings and money market accounts are low-risk options with lower returns compared to other investments. They provide liquidity and are FDIC-insured.

8. **Retirement Accounts (e.g., 401(k), IRA)**:

- **Description**: Retirement accounts are tax-advantaged investment accounts designed to help individuals save for retirement. They can hold a variety of investments, including stocks, bonds, and mutual funds.

- **Risk and Return**: The risk and return depend on the investments held within the account. Tax benefits and penalties for early withdrawal are considerations.

9. **Commodities**:

   - **Description**: Commodities are raw materials or primary agricultural products that can be bought and sold, such as gold, oil, agricultural products, etc.

   - **Risk and Return**: Commodity prices are influenced by supply and demand dynamics, geopolitical events, and economic factors. They offer potential for diversification but can be volatile.

Each type of investment has its own risk-return profile, suitability, and investment horizon. Diversification and understanding your risk tolerance and financial goals are key to building a well-rounded investment portfolio. It's advisable to consult with a financial advisor before making investment decisions.

RISK TOLERANCE AND INVESTMENT STRATEGIES

Understanding your risk tolerance is a crucial step in developing a suitable investment strategy. Risk tolerance refers to your ability and willingness to withstand fluctuations in the value of your investments. It's influenced by your financial goals, time horizon, investment knowledge, and comfort level with uncertainty. Matching your risk tolerance with an appropriate investment strategy can help you achieve your financial objectives while maintaining peace of mind. Here's how to determine risk tolerance and tailor investment strategies accordingly:

1. **Assess Your Risk Tolerance**:

a. **Risk Assessment Questionnaires**:

- Many financial institutions and online platforms offer risk assessment questionnaires. Answering a series of questions about your financial situation, goals, and attitudes toward risk helps determine your risk tolerance.

b. **Personal Reflection and Assessment**:

- Consider your emotional response to financial market fluctuations. Are you comfortable with potential ups and downs in your investments, or do market swings cause anxiety or concern?

- Evaluate your financial circumstances, including income, expenses, debt levels, emergency fund, and overall financial stability.

c. **Consult a Financial Advisor**:

- Seek advice from a financial advisor to assess your risk tolerance based on your financial situation, objectives, and comfort level with market volatility.

2. **Identify Your Investment Objectives**:

- **Short-Term Goals**: If you have short-term financial goals (e.g., buying a house, funding a vacation), consider investments with lower volatility and higher liquidity.

- **Long-Term Goals**: For long-term objectives like retirement or education funding, you can afford to take on more risk and invest in assets with potential for higher returns.

3. **Match Risk Tolerance with Investment Strategies**:

- **Conservative Risk Tolerance**:

- Investment Strategy: Focus on preserving capital and generating income with low-risk investments like bonds, CDs, money market accounts, and dividend-paying stocks.

- Characteristics: Lower potential returns, lower volatility, and a more cautious approach to market fluctuations.

- **Moderate Risk Tolerance**:

  - Investment Strategy: Diversify your portfolio with a mix of stocks, bonds, ETFs, and real estate investment trusts (REITs).

  - Characteristics: Balanced risk and return, moderate potential for growth, and a diversified approach.

- **Aggressive Risk Tolerance**:

  - Investment Strategy: Emphasize growth by investing in a higher proportion of stocks, including growth stocks, small-cap stocks, and international equities.

  - Characteristics: Higher potential returns, higher volatility, and a higher risk of short-term losses.

4. **Regularly Review and Adjust Your Portfolio**:

- **Rebalance Your Portfolio**: Periodically review your investments to ensure they align with your risk tolerance and financial goals. Rebalance your portfolio by adjusting asset allocations as needed.

- **Adjust Based on Life Changes**: Changes in your financial situation, goals, or risk tolerance should prompt adjustments to your investment strategy. Regularly revisit and realign your portfolio accordingly.

5. **Stay Informed and Seek Professional Advice**:

    - **Educate Yourself**: Stay informed about investment options, economic trends, and market conditions to make informed decisions that align with your risk tolerance.

    - **Consult Professionals**: Consider consulting a financial advisor to review and refine your investment strategy based on your evolving financial situation and goals.

By understanding your risk tolerance and aligning it with an appropriate investment strategy, you can build a diversified portfolio that maximizes potential returns while ensuring you remain comfortable with your investments, regardless of market conditions.

UNDERSTANDING RETIREMENT ACCOUNTS (401K, IRA)

Understanding retirement accounts like 401(k)s and IRAs (Individual Retirement Accounts) is essential for effective retirement planning. These accounts offer tax advantages and help individuals save and invest for their retirement years. Here's a detailed explanation of both:

1. **401(k) Retirement Account**:

    - **Description**: A 401(k) is an employer-sponsored retirement savings plan, where employees can contribute a portion of their pre-tax earnings into the account. Employers may also match a percentage of the employee's contributions.

    - **Contributions**: Contributions are made through payroll deductions and can be pre-tax (traditional 401(k)) or post-tax (Roth 401(k)). The 2021 and 2022 annual contribution limit is $19,500 for individuals under age 50, with an additional catch-up contribution of $6,500 for those 50 and older.

- **Tax Benefits**:

  - **Traditional 401(k)**: Contributions are tax-deferred, reducing current taxable income. You pay taxes upon withdrawal during retirement.

  - **Roth 401(k)**: Contributions are made after taxes, and qualified withdrawals, including earnings, are tax-free during retirement.

- **Investment Options**: 401(k) plans offer a range of investment options, such as stocks, bonds, mutual funds, ETFs, and more, based on the plan's design.

- **Withdrawals and Penalties**:

  - Withdrawals before age 59½ may incur a 10% early withdrawal penalty (with some exceptions).

  - Required Minimum Distributions (RMDs) must start by April 1 of the year following the year you turn 72 (or 70½ if you reached 70½ before January 1, 2020).

2. **Individual Retirement Account (IRA)**:

   - **Description**: An IRA is a tax-advantaged account that individuals can open independently, regardless of employer involvement. IRAs are provided by financial institutions and allow you to invest in various assets.

   - **Types of IRAs**:

- **Traditional IRA**: Contributions may be tax-deductible, and earnings grow tax-deferred. Taxes are paid upon withdrawal during retirement.

- **Roth IRA**: Contributions are made after taxes, and qualified withdrawals, including earnings, are tax-free during retirement.

- **SEP IRA**: Simplified Employee Pension IRA for self-employed individuals or small business owners.

- **Simple IRA**: Savings Incentive Match Plan for Employees for small businesses.

- **Contributions**: The 2021 and 2022 annual contribution limit is $6,000 for individuals under age 50, with an additional catch-up contribution of $1,000 for those 50 and older.

- **Tax Benefits and Eligibility**:

  - Tax benefits vary based on the type of IRA and your income level.

  - Income limits may affect eligibility and tax advantages for contributions to a Roth IRA or tax-deductible contributions to a traditional IRA.

- **Investment Options**: IRAs offer a broad range of investment options similar to those in a 401(k), depending on the financial institution where the IRA is held.

- **Withdrawals and Penalties**:

  - Withdrawals before age 59½ may incur a 10% early withdrawal penalty (with some exceptions).

  - Traditional IRA: Required Minimum Distributions (RMDs) must start by April 1 of the year following the year you turn 72 (or 70½ if you reached 70½ before January 1, 2020).

- Roth IRA: No required minimum distributions during the original account holder's lifetime.

Understanding the features, tax implications, and eligibility criteria of 401(k)s and IRAs is vital for effective retirement planning. It's advisable to consult a financial advisor to tailor a retirement strategy that aligns with your financial goals and circumstances.

RETIREMENT SAVINGS STRATEGIES AND OPTIONS

Saving for retirement is a critical financial goal, and employing effective strategies and exploring various options is essential to ensure a financially secure and comfortable retirement. Here are some retirement savings strategies and options to consider:

1. **Start Early and Maximize Contributions**:

   - Begin saving for retirement as early as possible to benefit from compounding over time. The earlier you start, the more time your investments have to grow.

   - Maximize your contributions to retirement accounts like 401(k)s, IRAs, or other employer-sponsored plans to take advantage of tax benefits and potential employer matches.

2. **Utilize Employer-Sponsored Retirement Plans**:

   - Take full advantage of employer-sponsored retirement plans like 401(k)s. Contribute enough to meet any employer match, as it's essentially free money added to your retirement savings.

3. **Contribute to Individual Retirement Accounts (IRAs)**:

- Contribute to both traditional and Roth IRAs, if eligible, to diversify tax advantages and maximize savings.

- Regularly contribute the annual maximum allowable amounts to these accounts to benefit from tax-deferred or tax-free growth.

4. **Consider a Health Savings Account (HSA)**:

   - If eligible, contribute to an HSA to save for medical expenses during retirement. HSAs offer triple tax advantages: tax-deductible contributions, tax-free growth, and tax-free withdrawals for qualified medical expenses.

5. **Automatic Contributions and Payroll Deductions**:

   - Set up automatic contributions to your retirement accounts, ensuring consistent and disciplined saving. Arrange for payroll deductions to contribute a portion of your salary directly to your retirement funds.

6. **Diversify Your Investments**:

   - Diversify your portfolio by investing in a mix of asset classes (e.g., stocks, bonds, real estate, commodities) based on your risk tolerance and time horizon.

   - Consider rebalancing your portfolio periodically to maintain the desired asset allocation and risk level.

7. **Catch-Up Contributions**:

   - If you're age 50 or older, take advantage of catch-up contributions allowed by retirement accounts. This enables you to contribute additional funds beyond the standard annual contribution limits.

8. **Delay Retirement or Work Part-Time**:

   - Consider delaying your retirement or working part-time during retirement to supplement your income and allow your retirement savings to grow further.

9. **Downsize or Relocate**:

   - Consider downsizing your home or relocating to a more affordable area during retirement to reduce living expenses and potentially unlock home equity to supplement your retirement savings.

10. **Explore Annuities and Pension Plans**:

    - Investigate annuities or pension plans that provide a steady stream of income during retirement, helping ensure financial security and peace of mind.

11. **Seek Professional Financial Advice**:

    - Consult a certified financial advisor to develop a tailored retirement savings strategy, considering your individual circumstances, risk tolerance, and financial goals.

12. **Regularly Review and Adjust Your Plan**:

    - Periodically review your retirement savings plan and adjust it based on changes in your financial situation, goals, and market conditions.

Remember, every individual's financial situation is unique, so it's crucial to customize your retirement savings strategy to align with your specific goals and circumstances. Planning for retirement early and being diligent in your savings and investment approach can significantly impact your financial security during your golden years.

PLANNING FOR A COMFORTABLE RETIREMENT

Planning for a comfortable retirement involves a comprehensive approach that considers your financial goals, lifestyle expectations, healthcare needs, and long-term financial security. Here are steps and strategies to help you plan for a comfortable retirement:

1. **Set Clear Retirement Goals**:

   - Determine your desired retirement lifestyle, including travel, hobbies, living arrangements, and any other activities you envision.

   - Estimate the costs associated with your retirement goals to establish a savings target.

2. **Assess Your Current Financial Situation**:

   - Calculate your current assets, liabilities, and net worth.

   - Analyze your cash flow, including income, expenses, and savings rate.

3. **Create a Budget and Financial Plan**:

   - Develop a budget that accounts for your daily expenses, debt repayment, savings, and investments.

   - Establish a financial plan that aligns with your retirement goals, incorporating strategies for saving, investing, tax optimization, and risk management.

4. **Determine Your Retirement Age and Timeline**:

   - Decide the age at which you intend to retire. Consider your health, job satisfaction, and financial readiness.

   - Plan your timeline for achieving your retirement savings goal, considering your retirement age and expected life expectancy.

5. **Maximize Retirement Account Contributions**:

   - Contribute the maximum allowable amounts to retirement accounts such as 401(k)s, IRAs, or similar plans available in your country to take advantage of tax benefits and employer matches.

6. **Diversify Your Investments**:

   - Create a diversified investment portfolio that aligns with your risk tolerance, time horizon, and financial goals.

   - Allocate your investments across various asset classes (e.g., stocks, bonds, real estate) to mitigate risks and optimize potential returns.

7. **Minimize Debt and Expenses**:

   - Aim to pay off high-interest debts before retirement to reduce financial burdens during your non-working years.

   - Adopt a frugal lifestyle, control unnecessary expenses, and prioritize essential spending to maximize savings.

8. **Plan for Healthcare and Insurance**:

   - Understand healthcare costs during retirement and account for them in your financial plan.

   - Explore Medicare or other health insurance options to ensure you have adequate coverage for medical expenses.

9. **Consider Long-Term Care and Estate Planning**:

- Evaluate the need for long-term care insurance or alternative arrangements to cover potential long-term care costs.

- Establish or update your estate plan, including wills, trusts, and beneficiaries, to protect your assets and ensure a smooth transfer of wealth.

10. **Stay Informed and Adapt Your Plan**:

- Stay updated on financial markets, tax laws, and retirement planning strategies to make informed decisions.

- Regularly review and adjust your retirement plan based on changes in your life circumstances, financial situation, and goals.

11. **Explore Additional Income Streams**:

- Consider other potential sources of income during retirement, such as part-time work, rental income, or starting a small business to supplement your retirement funds.

12. **Consult a Financial Advisor**:

- Seek guidance from a certified financial advisor who specializes in retirement planning to help tailor a comprehensive plan based on your needs and objectives.

By following these steps and staying disciplined in your savings and investment approach, you can work towards achieving a comfortable and financially secure retirement that aligns with your envisioned lifestyle and goals.

BASICS OF INCOME TAX

Understanding the basics of income tax is essential for managing your finances effectively and meeting your tax obligations. Income tax is a tax imposed by the government on individuals and entities based on their earnings. Here are the key components and concepts related to income tax:

1. **Types of Income**:

   - **Earned Income**: Income from wages, salaries, bonuses, commissions, and self-employment.

   - **Passive Income**: Earnings from investments like dividends, interest, and rental income.

   - **Portfolio Income**: Gains from selling investments, such as stocks or real estate.

   - **Business Income**: Profits earned from running a business or being self-employed.

2. **Taxable Income**:

   - **Gross Income**: Total income before any deductions or exemptions.

   - **Adjustments**: Certain deductions (e.g., student loan interest, contributions to retirement accounts) that reduce taxable income.

   - **Taxable Income**: Gross income minus allowable adjustments and deductions.

3. **Tax Deductions and Credits**:

   - **Deductions**: Expenses or contributions that reduce taxable income, like mortgage interest, medical expenses, and charitable donations.

   - **Tax Credits**: Direct reductions in the amount of tax owed, often provided for specific expenses (e.g., education, child care) or circumstances (e.g., low-income individuals).

4. **Tax Brackets and Rates**:

- **Tax Brackets**: Divisions that determine the tax rate applied to your taxable income. The higher your income, the higher the tax rate.

- **Marginal Tax Rate**: The tax rate on the last dollar of income earned, which helps calculate the impact of additional earnings on taxes.

5. **Filing Status**:

- **Single**: Unmarried individuals, divorced, or legally separated.

- **Married Filing Jointly**: Married couples filing a single tax return, combining their incomes and deductions.

- **Head of Household**: Unmarried individuals responsible for at least half the household costs and having a qualifying dependent.

- **Married Filing Separately**: Married couples filing separate tax returns.

6. **Tax Forms**:

- **Form W-2**: Provided by employers, summarizing annual wages and taxes withheld.

- **Form 1099**: Summarizes various types of income earned, such as interest, dividends, or freelance work.

- **Form 1040 (or 1040A, 1040EZ)**: Standard tax forms for filing your annual tax return.

7. **Tax Withholding and Payments**:

- **Withholding**: Employers deduct taxes from employees' paychecks based on their Form W-4 (Employee's Withholding Certificate).

- **Estimated Tax Payments**: Self-employed individuals and those with additional income sources must make estimated quarterly tax payments.

8. **Tax Planning**:

   - **Tax Efficiency**: Strategically managing your finances to minimize tax liability while maximizing savings and investments.

   - **Year-End Planning**: Assessing your tax situation and making necessary adjustments before the end of the tax year.

9. **Tax Deadlines**:

   - **Tax Year**: Generally follows the calendar year (January 1 to December 31).

   - **Tax Filing Deadline**: In the United States, typically April 15th, or the following business day if it falls on a weekend or holiday.

Understanding these basic components of income tax will help you navigate the tax system, fulfill your tax obligations, and potentially optimize your financial situation by legally minimizing your tax liability. It's advisable to consult a tax professional for personalized guidance based on your specific circumstances.

TAX-SAVING INVESTMENTS AND DEDUCTIONS

Tax-saving investments and deductions can significantly reduce your taxable income and overall tax liability. Utilizing these can lead to potential tax savings, helping you retain more of your earnings for future financial goals. Here are common tax-saving investments and deductions:

1. **Retirement Account Contributions**:

- **Traditional IRA Contributions**: Contributions to a traditional Individual Retirement Account (IRA) are tax-deductible in the year you make them, potentially reducing your taxable income.

- **401(k) and Similar Plans**: Contributions to employer-sponsored retirement plans like 401(k)s are typically tax-deductible, effectively reducing your taxable income.

2. **Health Savings Account (HSA)**:

- Contributions to an HSA are tax-deductible and can be used to pay for qualified medical expenses tax-free. HSAs offer triple tax benefits: tax-deductible contributions, tax-free growth, and tax-free withdrawals for medical expenses.

3. **Health Insurance Premiums**:

- Premiums paid for certain health insurance plans, such as a Health Maintenance Organization (HMO) or a Preferred Provider Organization (PPO), may be tax-deductible.

4. **Mortgage Interest and Property Taxes**:

- Mortgage interest and property tax payments on your primary residence are typically tax-deductible, potentially reducing your taxable income.

5. **Education Expenses**:

- **Student Loan Interest Deduction**: Interest paid on qualifying student loans may be tax-deductible, subject to income limits.

- **Tuition and Fees Deduction**: Certain education-related expenses, like tuition and fees, may be deductible, subject to eligibility criteria.

6. **Charitable Donations**:

- Contributions made to qualified charitable organizations are tax-deductible. Keep records and receipts for donations made throughout the year.

7. **Homeownership Benefits**:

    - **First-time Homebuyer Credit**: Qualifying first-time homebuyers may be eligible for a tax credit.

    - **Energy-Efficient Home Improvements**: Energy-efficient home improvements, like solar panels or energy-efficient windows, may qualify for tax credits.

8. **Child and Dependent Care Expenses**:

    - You may be eligible for a tax credit or deduction for qualifying child and dependent care expenses while you work or look for work.

9. **State and Local Taxes (SALT)**:

    - Depending on your tax jurisdiction, you may be able to deduct state and local income taxes or sales taxes from your federal taxable income.

10. **Small Business Deductions**:

    - If you are a small business owner or self-employed, various business-related expenses may be tax-deductible, including home office expenses, equipment, supplies, and business travel.

11. **Investment Losses**:

    - Capital losses from selling investments at a loss can be used to offset capital gains, reducing your overall tax liability.

12. **Tax Credits for Children**:

- The Child Tax Credit and the Additional Child Tax Credit provide tax relief for families with qualifying children.

13. **Lifetime Learning Credit and American Opportunity Credit**:

- Education-related tax credits for eligible higher education expenses.

Understanding and utilizing these tax-saving investments and deductions can help you optimize your tax position, reduce your tax liability, and increase your after-tax income. It's important to consult a tax advisor or financial professional to ensure you are leveraging these opportunities effectively based on your individual circumstances.

TAX-EFFICIENT FINANCIAL STRATEGIES

Tax-efficient financial strategies are essential for optimizing your overall financial plan by minimizing the impact of taxes on your income, investments, and estate. Implementing tax-efficient strategies can help you retain a larger portion of your earnings, grow your wealth, and plan for a secure financial future. Here are some key tax-efficient financial strategies:

1. **Utilize Tax-Advantaged Accounts**:

- Contribute to tax-advantaged retirement accounts like 401(k)s, IRAs, HSAs, and 529 plans. These accounts offer tax deductions, tax-deferred growth, or tax-free withdrawals for qualified expenses, providing significant tax benefits.

2. **Tax-Efficient Asset Location**:

- Allocate investments strategically across taxable, tax-deferred, and tax-free accounts to optimize tax efficiency. Generally, tax-inefficient investments (e.g., bonds with regular interest) are placed in tax-advantaged accounts, while tax-efficient investments (e.g., index funds, stocks) are placed in taxable accounts.

3. **Tax-Loss Harvesting**:

   - Offset capital gains by selling investments that have experienced losses. This can help reduce your overall capital gains tax liability.

4. **Long-Term Investing**:

   - Hold investments for the long term (over one year) to qualify for lower long-term capital gains tax rates. Short-term gains are typically taxed at higher ordinary income tax rates.

5. **Dividend and Interest Income**:

   - Invest in tax-efficient funds or securities that generate qualified dividends or tax-free interest, which may receive preferential tax treatment.

6. **Roth Conversions and Backdoor Roth IRAs**:

   - Consider converting traditional IRA funds to a Roth IRA, paying taxes upfront to potentially enjoy tax-free withdrawals in retirement. High-income earners can utilize the backdoor Roth IRA strategy to contribute indirectly to a Roth IRA.

7. **Tax-Efficient Withdrawal Strategies**:

   - Plan your retirement withdrawals to minimize taxes by carefully selecting which accounts to draw from based on tax implications and your overall tax situation.

8. **Estate Planning and Gifting**:

- Implement tax-efficient estate planning strategies, such as gifting, trusts, and leveraging the estate tax exemption, to minimize estate taxes and efficiently transfer wealth to heirs.

9. **Tax Credits and Deductions**:

- Take advantage of available tax credits and deductions, such as those for education expenses, homeownership, energy-efficient improvements, and healthcare expenses.

10. **Timing of Deductions and Income**:

- Consider timing strategies like bunching deductions in specific years and managing your income to optimize your tax situation, especially in fluctuating income years.

11. **Investment in Municipal Bonds**:

- Invest in municipal bonds, which offer tax-free interest income at the federal level and often at the state and local levels.

12. **Consult a Tax Advisor**:

- Work with a tax professional or financial advisor with tax expertise to develop personalized tax-efficient strategies tailored to your financial goals and circumstances.

Regularly reviewing and adjusting your financial plan to align with changes in tax laws, your financial situation, and your goals is essential to ensure your tax-efficiency remains optimized over time. It's important to integrate tax planning into your overall financial strategy to achieve the best possible outcomes.

TYPES OF INSURANCE (LIFE, HEALTH, AUTO, HOME)

Insurance is a financial tool that provides protection against specific risks and uncertainties. Different types of insurance are designed to cover various aspects of your life and assets. Here are the main types of insurance:

1. **Life Insurance**:

   - **Term Life Insurance**: Provides coverage for a specific period (term) and pays out a death benefit if the insured passes away during the term.

   - **Whole Life Insurance**: Offers lifelong coverage and includes a savings or investment component, accumulating cash value over time.

   - **Universal Life Insurance**: Combines a death benefit with a savings component, allowing flexible premium payments and death benefit options.

   - **Variable Life Insurance**: Combines a death benefit with an investment component, allowing the policyholder to invest in various options (e.g., stocks, bonds) within the policy.

2. **Health Insurance**:

   - **Health Maintenance Organization (HMO)**: Requires individuals to choose a primary care physician and obtain referrals for specialists.

   - **Preferred Provider Organization (PPO)**: Offers more flexibility in choosing healthcare providers and specialists without referrals.

   - **Point of Service (POS)**: Combines features of HMO and PPO plans, allowing both in-network and out-of-network coverage.

- **High Deductible Health Plan (HDHP)**: Features higher deductibles and lower premiums, often paired with Health Savings Accounts (HSAs) for tax advantages.

3. **Auto Insurance**:

   - **Liability Insurance**: Covers bodily injury and property damage you may cause to others in an accident.

   - **Collision Coverage**: Pays for damage to your own vehicle from a collision with another vehicle or object.

   - **Comprehensive Coverage**: Protects against non-collision events, such as theft, vandalism, natural disasters, or hitting an animal.

   - **Uninsured/Underinsured Motorist Coverage**: Covers you if you're in an accident with a driver who doesn't have insurance or sufficient coverage.

4. **Homeowners Insurance**:

   - **Dwelling Coverage**: Protects your home's structure, including walls, roof, and attached structures.

   - **Personal Property Coverage**: Covers personal belongings inside your home, like furniture, electronics, and clothing.

   - **Liability Coverage**: Provides protection if someone is injured on your property or if you damage someone else's property.

   - **Additional Living Expenses (ALE)**: Covers living expenses if you're temporarily displaced from your home due to a covered event.

5. **Renters Insurance**:

- **Personal Property Coverage**: Protects personal belongings, including electronics, clothing, furniture, and more.

- **Liability Coverage**: Covers liability for injuries or damages to others that occur within your rented space.

- **Loss of Use Coverage**: Pays for additional living expenses if you're temporarily unable to stay in your rented home due to a covered event.

6. **Disability Insurance**:

   - **Short-Term Disability Insurance**: Provides income replacement for a short period if you're unable to work due to a temporary disability.

   - **Long-Term Disability Insurance**: Offers income replacement for an extended period if you're unable to work due to a long-term disability.

7. **Travel Insurance**:

   - **Trip Cancellation and Interruption Insurance**: Reimburses non-refundable trip expenses if your trip is canceled or cut short due to covered reasons.

   - **Medical and Evacuation Insurance**: Covers medical emergencies and evacuation during travel.

   - **Baggage and Personal Belongings Insurance**: Protects against lost, damaged, or stolen luggage and personal items during the trip.

Understanding the different types of insurance and their coverage options is crucial for making informed decisions to protect yourself, your loved ones, and your assets in various life situations. It's important to assess your needs and consult with insurance professionals to determine the most appropriate coverage for your circumstances.

SELECTING APPROPRIATE INSURANCE COVERAGE

Selecting appropriate insurance coverage is a critical step in safeguarding your finances, health, assets, and loved ones from various risks and uncertainties. Here's a step-by-step guide to help you choose the right insurance coverage for your specific needs:

1. **Assess Your Needs and Risks**:

    - **Analyze Your Life Stage and Situation**: Consider factors such as age, health, family situation, employment, and financial status to determine your insurance needs.

    - **Identify Potential Risks**: Recognize the risks you face, such as accidents, illness, property damage, liability, or loss of income.

2. **Understand Types of Insurance**:

    - **Research Different Types of Insurance**: Learn about the various types of insurance available, including life, health, auto, home, renters, disability, travel, etc.

    - **Understand Coverage and Exclusions**: Familiarize yourself with what each type of insurance covers and any exclusions or limitations.

3. **Assess Existing Coverage**:

    - **Review Employer-Provided Insurance**: If applicable, assess insurance coverage provided by your employer (e.g., health, life, disability).

    - **Evaluate Existing Policies**: Review any current insurance policies you have to determine if they meet your current needs or require adjustments.

4. **Determine Coverage Amounts and Limits**:

   - **Evaluate Your Assets and Liabilities**: Consider the value of your home, vehicles, savings, investments, outstanding debts, and future financial obligations.

   - **Calculate Potential Losses**: Estimate potential financial losses from various risks to determine appropriate coverage amounts.

5. **Consider Deductibles and Premiums**:

   - **Balance Deductibles and Premiums**: Understand how deductibles and premiums affect your insurance costs. Higher deductibles often result in lower premiums but higher out-of-pocket expenses.

6. **Compare Multiple Insurance Quotes**:

   - **Request Quotes from Multiple Providers**: Obtain quotes from several reputable insurance companies to compare coverage options, prices, deductibles, and customer service.

   - **Consider Independent Agents**: Consult independent insurance agents who can provide options from multiple insurers, helping you find the best coverage at the most competitive rates.

7. **Read and Understand Policies Thoroughly**:

   - **Review Policy Terms and Conditions**: Carefully read and understand the terms, conditions, coverage limits, exclusions, and any endorsements or riders associated with the policy.

8. **Check Insurance Company Ratings and Reputation**:

- **Research Financial Strength**: Check the financial stability and credit ratings of the insurance companies to ensure they can meet their financial obligations.

- **Read Customer Reviews and Testimonials**: Look for reviews and feedback from policyholders to gauge customer satisfaction and the company's reputation.

9. **Seek Professional Guidance**:

- **Consult Insurance Professionals**: Consider seeking advice from insurance brokers, financial advisors, or insurance consultants to help you navigate policy options and select appropriate coverage.

10. **Regularly Review and Update Your Coverage**:

- **Periodic Reviews**: Reevaluate your insurance needs periodically, especially after significant life events, to ensure your coverage aligns with your current circumstances and risks.

Choosing the right insurance coverage requires careful consideration of your individual needs, thorough research, and informed decision-making. Take the time to assess your risks and reach out to professionals for guidance to ensure you have the appropriate coverage in place.

MANAGING FINANCIAL RISKS

Managing financial risks is a crucial aspect of maintaining financial stability and achieving your long-term financial goals. Financial risks can arise from various sources, including market volatility, economic fluctuations, unexpected expenses, health issues, or changes in personal circumstances. Here are effective strategies to manage financial risks:

1. **Build an Emergency Fund**:

- Establish an emergency fund with at least three to six months' worth of living expenses to cover unexpected financial setbacks, such as medical emergencies or job loss.

2. **Insurance Coverage**:

- Obtain appropriate insurance coverage (e.g., life, health, property, liability, disability) to protect yourself, your family, and your assets from unforeseen events and potential financial losses.

3. **Diversify Investments**:

- Diversify your investment portfolio across different asset classes (e.g., stocks, bonds, real estate) to spread risk and minimize the impact of market fluctuations on your overall investments.

4. **Risk Tolerance Assessment**:

- Assess your risk tolerance and align your investment choices accordingly. Invest in a manner that matches your risk tolerance and financial goals to prevent excessive exposure to market volatility.

5. **Regular Portfolio Rebalancing**:

- Periodically review and rebalance your investment portfolio to ensure it remains aligned with your risk tolerance and financial objectives. Rebalancing helps manage risks and maintain a diversified portfolio.

6. **Long-Term Financial Planning**:

- Develop a comprehensive financial plan that considers your short-term and long-term goals, risk tolerance, and time horizon. Regularly revisit and update the plan to reflect changes in your circumstances.

7. **Debt Management**:

- Manage and minimize debt by establishing a budget, prioritizing debt repayment, and avoiding high-interest debt. Debt reduction enhances financial stability and reduces financial risk.

8. **Tax Planning and Compliance**:

- Engage in tax planning to optimize tax efficiency and reduce tax liabilities. Ensure compliance with tax laws and regulations to avoid penalties and unexpected tax burdens.

9. **Education and Information**:

- Stay informed about financial markets, economic trends, and changes in legislation that may impact your finances. Educate yourself on investment options, insurance products, and financial planning strategies.

10. **Professional Financial Advice**:

- Seek guidance from certified financial advisors or planners to develop a personalized risk management strategy that aligns with your financial goals and risk tolerance.

11. **Scenario Analysis and Stress Testing**:

- Conduct scenario analysis and stress tests on your financial plan and investment portfolio to assess how different economic conditions or events might impact your financial position. Use these insights to make informed decisions and mitigate potential risks.

12. **Crisis and Contingency Planning**:

   - Develop contingency plans for unexpected events such as economic downturns, natural disasters, or health emergencies. Consider how you would adjust your finances and lifestyle during challenging times.

By employing these strategies and maintaining a proactive approach to risk management, you can effectively navigate financial risks and work towards achieving your financial aspirations while safeguarding your financial well-being.

BUYING VS. RENTING A HOME

The decision to buy or rent a home depends on various factors, including your financial situation, lifestyle, housing market conditions, and long-term goals. Both options have their advantages and considerations. Here's a comparison to help you weigh the pros and cons:

Buying a Home:

1. **Equity and Asset Building**:

   - **Pros**: Homeownership builds equity, which can be used for future investments, upgrades, or as a source of financing.

   - **Cons**: Initial costs and fees can be high, and the rate of equity growth may vary based on the real estate market.

2. **Stability and Control**:

- **Pros**: You have control over the property, allowing customization, improvements, and stability in a community.

- **Cons**: Responsibilities include maintenance, repairs, property taxes, and homeowners association (HOA) fees.

3. **Tax Benefits**:

- **Pros**: Mortgage interest and property tax deductions can result in tax advantages, potentially reducing your overall tax liability.

- **Cons**: You need to itemize deductions, and the tax benefits may vary based on tax laws and individual circumstances.

4. **Predictable Payments**:

- **Pros**: Fixed-rate mortgages offer predictable monthly payments over the loan term, providing stability and ease in budgeting.

- **Cons**: Initial costs may be high, and property taxes or insurance costs can change over time.

5. **Long-Term Investment**:

- **Pros**: Historically, real estate tends to appreciate over time, offering the potential for a profitable long-term investment.

- **Cons**: Market conditions can fluctuate, affecting property values and potential returns.

Renting a Home:

1. **Flexibility and Mobility**:

- **Pros**: Renting provides the flexibility to relocate easily for career opportunities or lifestyle changes without the burden of selling a property.

- **Cons**: Rent increases or lease terms may affect long-term housing costs.

2. **Lower Initial Costs**:

   - **Pros**: Renting typically requires lower upfront costs, such as a security deposit and sometimes the first and last month's rent.

   - **Cons**: You don't build equity or accumulate long-term assets through renting.

3. **Maintenance and Repairs**:

   - **Pros**: Landlords are typically responsible for property maintenance, saving you from unexpected repair costs.

   - **Cons**: Limited control over property modifications or improvements.

4. **Financial Flexibility**:

   - **Pros**: Renting allows you to allocate savings toward investments, travel, or other financial goals without tying up funds in a property.

   - **Cons**: Rent payments do not contribute to homeownership or equity building.

5. **Market Exposure and Market Timing**:

   - **Pros**: Renting lets you observe local real estate market trends, helping you decide when and where to buy if you choose to do so.

   - **Cons**: Market conditions can influence rent prices and availability, affecting housing options.

Considerations:

- **Market Conditions**: Assess the local real estate market, property values, and rental rates.

- **Financial Stability**: Evaluate your financial health, credit score, and ability to secure a mortgage.

- **Lifestyle and Future Plans**: Consider your future plans, job stability, family growth, and how a housing choice aligns with these plans.

In summary, buying a home offers long-term stability, equity building, and potential tax benefits, but it comes with responsibilities and upfront costs. Renting provides flexibility and lower initial costs but lacks the long-term financial benefits associated with homeownership. Your decision should align with your financial goals, lifestyle preferences, and long-term plans. Consulting with a financial advisor can also help you make an informed decision based on your specific circumstances.

UNDERSTANDING MORTGAGES AND FINANCING OPTIONS

Understanding mortgages and financing options is crucial when considering buying a home. A mortgage is a loan specifically used to purchase real estate, and it's typically repaid over a specified period with interest. Here's an overview of mortgages and various financing options:

1. Types of Mortgages:

1. **Fixed-Rate Mortgage (FRM)**:

   - **Pros**: Offers a stable interest rate and monthly payments throughout the loan term, making budgeting predictable.

   - **Cons**: Initial interest rates might be higher than adjustable-rate mortgages.

2. **Adjustable-Rate Mortgage (ARM)**:

- **Pros**: Initial interest rates are often lower than fixed-rate mortgages, allowing lower initial payments.

- **Cons**: Interest rates and payments can increase over time, leading to uncertainty.

3. **FHA Loans (Federal Housing Administration)**:

   - **Pros**: Requires lower down payments and may be available to individuals with lower credit scores.

   - **Cons**: Requires mortgage insurance premiums (MIP) for down payments less than 20%.

4. **VA Loans (U.S. Department of Veterans Affairs)**:

   - **Pros**: Available to eligible veterans, active-duty service members, and certain members of the National Guard and Reserves with no down payment and no private mortgage insurance (PMI) requirement.

   - **Cons**: Limited to eligible service members and veterans.

5. **USDA Loans (U.S. Department of Agriculture)**:

   - **Pros**: Designed for eligible rural and suburban homebuyers with no down payment requirement.

   - **Cons**: Limited to specific rural areas and income eligibility.

6. **Interest-Only Mortgage**:

   - **Pros**: Allows interest-only payments for a certain period (e.g., 5-10 years), lowering initial payments.

- **Cons**: Principal balance remains unchanged during the interest-only period and doesn't build home equity.

7. **Jumbo Loans**:

   - **Pros**: Allow higher loan amounts for properties exceeding conforming loan limits.

   - **Cons**: Typically require higher credit scores, down payments, and interest rates.

2. Key Financing Concepts:

1. **Down Payment**:

   - The upfront payment made by the buyer, expressed as a percentage of the home's purchase price. A larger down payment can lead to better loan terms and lower monthly payments.

2. **Loan Term**:

   - The duration of the loan repayment period (e.g., 15, 20, 30 years). Shorter terms typically have higher monthly payments but lower interest costs over the life of the loan.

3. **Interest Rate**:

   - The percentage of the loan amount that the lender charges annually for borrowing the money. It significantly impacts your monthly payments and the overall cost of the loan.

4. **Closing Costs**:

   - Various fees and expenses associated with finalizing the mortgage, typically including appraisal fees, title insurance, attorney fees, and more.

5. **Private Mortgage Insurance (PMI)**:

   - Insurance that protects the lender in case the borrower defaults on the loan. Usually required for down payments less than 20%.

6. **Amortization**:

   - The process of paying off the loan through regular payments over the loan term, consisting of both principal and interest.

7. **Preapproval vs. Prequalification**:

   - **Prequalification**: An informal estimate of how much you may be able to borrow based on basic financial information.

   - **Preapproval**: A more comprehensive evaluation of your financial background, providing a conditional commitment for a specific loan amount.

3. Choosing the Right Mortgage:

- Evaluate your financial situation, including credit score, income, debt-to-income ratio, and down payment capacity.

- Compare interest rates, loan terms, and total costs (including closing costs and PMI) from multiple lenders.

- Consider consulting a mortgage broker or financial advisor to explore various options and determine the most suitable mortgage for your needs.

Understanding mortgages and financing options empowers you to make informed decisions when choosing a loan that aligns with your financial goals and circumstances. It's essential to carefully consider the terms, costs, and long-term implications of any mortgage before making a commitment.

HOME OWNERSHIP AND ITS FINANCIAL IMPLICATIONS

Homeownership is a significant financial decision that comes with various implications and considerations. It's important to thoroughly understand the financial aspects associated with owning a home to make informed choices. Here are key financial implications of homeownership:

1. Initial Costs:

- **Down Payment**: An upfront payment made towards the purchase price of the home, typically a percentage of the total price (e.g., 5%, 10%, 20%).

- **Closing Costs**: Various fees and charges associated with finalizing the home purchase, including loan origination fees, attorney fees, title insurance, appraisal fees, and more.

2. Mortgage Financing:

- **Monthly Mortgage Payments**: Regular payments made to the lender to repay the loan, including principal and interest.

- **Interest Rates**: The interest charged on the mortgage significantly affects the overall cost of homeownership. It's crucial to obtain a competitive interest rate.

- **Loan Term**: The length of time to repay the mortgage (e.g., 15, 20, 30 years). Shorter terms typically have higher monthly payments but lower total interest paid.

- **Amortization**: The process of paying down the loan balance over time through regular mortgage payments.

3. Homeownership Expenses:

- **Property Taxes**: Taxes paid to the local government based on the assessed value of the property.

- **Homeowners Insurance**: Insurance that covers damage or loss to the property and its contents.

- **Maintenance and Repairs**: Ongoing costs to maintain the property, including repairs, utilities, and general maintenance.

- **Homeowners Association (HOA) Fees**: Regular fees paid to a homeowners association for shared community expenses and amenities.

4. Equity and Investment:

- **Equity Buildup**: As you pay down the mortgage, you build equity, which is the portion of the home you own outright.

- **Home Appreciation**: Historically, homes tend to appreciate in value over time, potentially providing a return on investment when you sell.

5. Tax Implications:

- **Tax Deductions**: Homeowners may qualify for tax deductions on mortgage interest, property taxes, and certain home-related expenses.

- **Capital Gains Tax Exclusion**: Homeowners may exclude a portion of capital gains from the sale of their primary residence (up to certain limits) from taxable income.

6. Leveraging Home Equity:

- **Home Equity Loans and Lines of Credit**: Homeowners can use home equity for loans or lines of credit, often with favorable interest rates, to fund various expenses like home improvements, education, or debt consolidation.

7. Market Fluctuations and Risks:

- **Real Estate Market Conditions**: Changes in property values and market trends can affect your home's value and potential return on investment.

- **Foreclosure Risk**: If unable to make mortgage payments, there's a risk of foreclosure and potential loss of the home.

8. Retirement and Estate Planning:

- **Long-Term Financial Planning**: Owning a home can be part of your retirement strategy, as paying off the mortgage can contribute to a debt-free retirement.

- **Estate Value and Inheritance**: The value of your home and how it factors into your estate plan and potential inheritance for heirs.

9. Considerations for Future Moves:

- **Selling and Moving Costs**: Costs associated with selling the home, including real estate agent commissions and moving expenses.

- **Buying a New Home**: Financing and costs associated with purchasing a new home if you decide to move.

10. Opportunity Costs:

- **Tying Up Capital**: Money invested in a home is not readily available for other investments, potentially impacting diversification and overall financial portfolio growth.

Owning a home offers stability, potential financial growth through equity and appreciation, and the opportunity to build a sense of community. However, it's crucial to carefully consider the financial implications and responsibilities associated with homeownership to ensure it aligns with your financial goals and circumstances. Consulting with financial advisors and real estate professionals can provide valuable insights and guidance in navigating the financial aspects of homeownership.

UTILIZING EDUCAITON RESOURCES FOR COTINUOUS LEARNING

Utilizing educational resources for continuous learning is a valuable strategy to enhance your knowledge, skills, and professional development. Lifelong learning keeps you updated with the latest advancements in your field and helps you adapt to evolving trends. Here's a guide on effectively utilizing educational resources for continuous learning:

1. Identify Learning Goals:

- **Self-Assessment**: Evaluate your current skills, knowledge gaps, and areas for improvement to determine your learning objectives.

- **Long-term Goals**: Align your learning goals with your long-term career objectives and personal growth aspirations.

2. Explore Diverse Learning Platforms:

- **Online Courses and Platforms**:

  - Websites like Coursera, edX, Udemy, and Khan Academy offer a wide range of courses in various subjects.

- **E-Libraries and Online Books**:

  - Platforms like Google Books, Project Gutenberg, and Open Library provide access to a vast collection of digital books.

- **Educational YouTube Channels and Podcasts**:

- Subscribe to relevant YouTube channels and podcasts that offer educational content in your area of interest.

- **Professional Associations and Organizations**:

  - Many professional associations provide online courses, webinars, and workshops to keep members updated with industry trends.

3. Establish a Learning Routine:

- **Set Aside Time**: Allocate dedicated time in your schedule for learning activities, whether it's daily, weekly, or monthly.

- **Consistency**: Be consistent in your learning routine to make it a habit and maximize knowledge retention.

4. Engage in Interactive Learning:

- **Participate in Online Communities and Forums**:

  - Engage in discussions, ask questions, and share insights with peers in relevant online communities related to your field of study.

- **Collaborate on Projects**: Work on collaborative projects or group assignments to apply your knowledge and learn from others.

5. Utilize Free and Open-Source Resources:

- **Open Educational Resources (OER)**:

  - Explore open-access textbooks, lecture notes, and educational materials available for free or at minimal cost.

- **Blogs and Online Articles**:

  - Follow reputable blogs and online publications related to your field to stay informed about current topics and research.

6. Incorporate Practical Applications:

- **Apply Knowledge at Work**: Integrate what you've learned into your professional activities and projects to enhance your skills and contribute to your workplace.

- **Personal Projects**: Undertake personal projects related to your area of interest to reinforce your learning and gain hands-on experience.

7. Track Progress and Reflect:

- **Keep a Learning Journal**: Document your learning journey, progress, challenges faced, and insights gained. Regularly review and reflect on your growth.

- **Assess Learning Outcomes**: Evaluate your progress against your learning goals to identify areas of improvement and adjust your learning strategy if needed.

8. Seek Mentorship and Guidance:

- **Mentorship Programs**: Engage with mentors in your field who can provide guidance, advice, and a structured approach to your learning journey.

- **Networking**: Build a professional network and seek advice from experienced individuals in your field to gain diverse perspectives.

9. Stay Updated with Industry Trends:

- **Follow Thought Leaders and Influencers**: Keep track of thought leaders in your field by following them on social media, reading their publications, or attending their webinars.

- **Subscribe to Newsletters and Journals**: Stay informed about the latest trends, research, and developments through industry newsletters, academic journals, and reputable news sources.

Continuous learning is a powerful tool for personal and professional growth. By leveraging a variety of educational resources and adopting a proactive and structured approach to learning, you can enhance your knowledge and skills throughout your career.

SEEKING FINANCIAL ADVICE AND GUIDANCE

Seeking financial advice and guidance is a prudent step to take control of your finances, plan for the future, and achieve your financial goals. Here's a comprehensive guide on how to seek and make the most of financial advice:

1. Define Your Financial Goals and Needs:

- **Short-Term and Long-Term Goals**: Clearly articulate your short-term (e.g., paying off debt) and long-term (e.g., retirement, buying a house) financial goals.

- **Assess Your Financial Situation**: Evaluate your income, expenses, assets, liabilities, insurance coverage, and investments to understand your financial health.

2. Choose the Right Financial Advisor:

- **Certifications and Credentials**: Look for advisors with relevant certifications such as Certified Financial Planner (CFP), Chartered Financial Analyst (CFA), or Certified Public Accountant (CPA).

- **Experience and Expertise**: Consider advisors with a proven track record in areas that align with your needs, whether it's investment management, tax planning, or retirement planning.

- **Fee Structure**: Understand how the advisor charges fees—whether it's fee-only, fee-based, commission-based, or a combination. Choose a transparent fee structure that aligns with your preferences.

3. Seek Recommendations and Do Research:

- **Ask for Recommendations**: Seek referrals from trusted friends, family, or colleagues who have had positive experiences with financial advisors.

- **Online Reviews and Ratings**: Check online reviews and ratings for financial advisors to get a sense of their reputation and service quality.

4. Have an Initial Consultation:

- **Ask Relevant Questions**: During the consultation, inquire about the advisor's approach, services offered, investment philosophy, and how they tailor advice to clients.

- **Discuss Fees and Costs**: Clarify the fee structure, any potential conflicts of interest, and ensure you are comfortable with the costs involved.

5. Review and Understand the Financial Plan:

- **Thoroughly Review the Plan**: If the advisor creates a financial plan, carefully review all components, assumptions, recommendations, and strategies outlined in the plan.

- **Ask Questions for Clarity**: Don't hesitate to ask for clarification on any aspect of the plan that you don't fully understand.

6. Establish a Relationship and Communicate Regularly:

- **Regular Check-Ins**: Maintain regular communication with your advisor to update them on any changes in your financial situation, goals, or risk tolerance.

- **Stay Informed**: Educate yourself about basic financial concepts to engage in meaningful discussions with your advisor and make informed decisions.

7. Be Open and Honest:

- **Provide Comprehensive Information**: Share all relevant financial information and details with your advisor, even if it seems minor. Complete transparency helps in creating an accurate financial plan.

- **Express Your Concerns**: If you have any concerns or uncertainties, be open about them with your advisor. Clear communication is essential for a successful advisory relationship.

8. Monitor Progress and Adjust as Needed:

- **Track Your Progress**: Regularly review your financial plan and investment performance to ensure you are on track to meet your goals.

- **Be Open to Adjustments**: Be flexible and willing to adjust your financial plan and investments based on changing circumstances, market conditions, or life events.

9. Educate Yourself Continuously:

- **Read Books and Articles**: Stay updated with financial literature to broaden your knowledge about personal finance, investments, and financial planning.

- **Attend Workshops and Seminars**: Participate in workshops, webinars, or seminars related to financial literacy and wealth management.

10. Exercise Caution and Due Diligence:

- **Verify Recommendations**: Cross-check recommendations and advice received from advisors to ensure they align with your financial goals and needs.

- **Avoid High-Pressure Sales Tactics**: Be wary of advisors who use aggressive sales techniques or pressure you into making rushed decisions.

11. Consider a Second Opinion:

- **Consult Multiple Advisors**: If needed, seek a second opinion from another reputable financial advisor to validate the recommendations you've received.

- **Compare Advice**: Compare the advice given by both advisors to make an informed decision.

12. Take Responsibility for Your Finances:

- **Stay Involved and Informed**: While seeking advice is essential, remember that ultimately, you are responsible for your financial decisions. Stay engaged and proactive in managing your finances.

By following these steps and being proactive in managing your finances, you'll be well-equipped to seek and utilize financial advice effectively. A solid relationship with a trusted financial advisor can greatly contribute to your financial success and overall peace of mind.

ONLINE TOOLS AND COMMUNITIES FOR FINANCIAL LITERACY

Embracing online tools and communities for financial literacy can greatly enhance your understanding of personal finance, investments, budgeting, and more. These resources provide valuable insights, interactive platforms, and opportunities for discussions. Here are some popular online tools and communities for financial literacy:

Online Tools:

1. **Mint**:

   - **Website**: Mint

- **Description**: A popular budgeting tool that helps you track expenses, create budgets, and set financial goals.

2. **Personal Capital**:

   - **Website**: Personal Capital

   - **Description**: An online platform that offers tools for tracking and managing investments, creating budgets, and planning for retirement.

3. **YNAB (You Need a Budget)**:

   - **Website**: YNAB

   - **Description**: Focuses on budgeting and managing your money to allocate funds effectively for all your expenses.

4. **Credit Karma**:

   - **Website**: Credit Karma

   - **Description**: Allows you to check your credit scores, monitor credit reports, and provides tips on improving your credit health.

5. **Investopedia**:

   - **Website**: Investopedia

   - **Description**: Offers a vast array of educational articles, tutorials, and financial terms to help you understand finance and investing.

6. **Morningstar**:

   - **Website**: Morningstar

- **Description**: Provides investment research, analysis, and portfolio tracking tools to help you make informed investment decisions.

7. **Bankrate**:

   - **Website**: Bankrate

   - **Description**: Offers financial advice, calculators, and comparison tools for loans, mortgages, credit cards, and more.

8. **Robo-Advisors (e.g., Betterment, Wealthfront)**:

   - **Description**: Online investment platforms that provide automated investment management services based on your risk tolerance and financial goals.

Online Communities and Forums:

1. **Reddit Finance Communities**:

   - **Subreddits**: Such as r/personalfinance, r/investing, and r/financialindependence offer a platform for discussions, advice, and sharing experiences with a vast community of users.

2. **Bogleheads Forum**:

   - **Website**: Bogleheads Forum

   - **Description**: A community focused on discussing investment strategies inspired by the philosophy of John Bogle, the founder of Vanguard.

3. **The White Coat Investor Forum**:

   - **Website**: The White Coat Investor Forum

- **Description**: Geared towards physicians and other high-income professionals, discussing various financial topics and strategies.

4. **Stack Exchange - Personal Finance & Money**:

   - **Website**: Stack Exchange - Personal Finance & Money

   - **Description**: An active community where you can ask and answer questions related to personal finance and money management.

5. **Facebook Groups**:

   - Various groups dedicated to personal finance, investing, budgeting, and financial literacy. Examples include "ChooseFI," "Dave Ramsey Fans," and "The Financial Diet Community."

6. **LinkedIn Groups**:

   - Join groups like "Financial Planning Association," "Personal Finance & Investment Professionals," and more to engage with professionals and enthusiasts in the finance industry.

7. **Quora - Personal Finance Section**:

   - **Website**: Quora - Personal Finance

   - **Description**: An online platform where you can ask questions related to personal finance and get answers from experts and the community.

These online tools and communities provide a wealth of information, interactive platforms, and access to knowledgeable individuals who can assist you in enhancing your financial literacy and making informed financial decisions. It's important to choose the resources that align with your learning

objectives and preferences.